HOW TO

Connect

HOW TO

Connect

CHRIS SHIPLEY

With illustrations by
STEPH BRADSHAW

ZIFF-DAVIS PRESS
EMERYVILLE, CALIFORNIA

Development Editor	Valerie Haynes Perry
Copy Editor	Noelle Graney
Technical Reviewer	Bob Flanders
Project Coordinator	A. Knox
Proofreaders	A. Knox and Noelle Graney
Cover Illustration	Steph Bradshaw
Cover Design	Carrie English
Book Design	Dennis Gallagher/Visual Strategies, San Francisco
Technical Illustration	Steph Bradshaw and Cherie Plumlee Computer Graphics & Illustration
Assistant Illustrators	Mary Pezzuto and Tony Jonick
Word Processing	Howard Blechman and Cat Haglund
Page Layout	Tony Jonick and M. D. Barrera
Indexer	Carol Burbo

Ziff-Davis Press books are produced on a Macintosh computer system with the following applications: FrameMaker®, Microsoft® Word, QuarkXPress®, Adobe Illustrator®, Adobe Photoshop®, Adobe Streamline™, MacLink® Plus, Aldus® FreeHand™, Collage Plus™.

Ziff-Davis Press
5903 Christie Avenue
Emeryville, CA 94608
1-800-688-0448

ISBN 1-56276-175-7

Manufactured in the United States of America
10 9 8 7 6 5 4 3 2 1

To the memory of Debbie Shipley Redfoot, a wonderful person who knew better than most how to connect.

TABLE OF CONTENTS

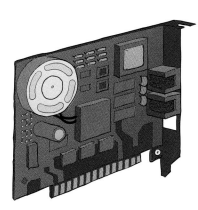

ACKNOWLEDGMENTS

I'm no fan of long, awkward public acknowledgments of things that are better shared personally. Yet necessarily I must spend a few words here to say thanks as best I can to those who made this book come together as well as it did.

I could never have been in the place to do a book such as this if not for my colleagues at Ziff Desktop Information. I especially thank Ed Passarella for getting me into this on-line business and for quietly giving me the time to get this book done, and Michael DeNitto for revealing the secrets of Prodigy screen capture and other interesting things.

I owe much to the people on the ZD Press team who brought such energy, enthusiasm, and creativity to this project, especially Valerie Haynes Perry for her insights and encouragements, Bob Flanders for his careful and (could it be true?) delightful tech edits, Steph Bradshaw for his wonderful illustrations, Cherie Plumlee for rendering screen images that clearly communicate what's going on, and Cindy Hudson for inviting me to do this book in the first place.

There are not enough thank yous in the world for Kristin Woolever, who showed me tremendous patience through a long summer of nights and weekends working, writing, and worrying. I'm eager, now, to catch up on all I've missed in the last months.

INTRODUCTION

You are holding in your hands the key that unlocks the fantastic world of on-line communications. It is a world that is both vast and small. Vast because on-line networks span the globe. Vast because on line there is no imaginable information that you can't find. Vast because on-line services bring together millions and millions of people. Yet, the on-line world is small, too. Small because on-line services really are intimate communities of people of like interests. Small because on line shrinks the distance and erases the boundaries between people and places around the world. Small because on-line services can meet exactly your personal expectations.

Yes, this book is the key to open that world. It will not just tell, but also show you step-by-step everything you need to know to open the door to on-line communications. It will guide you start to finish through creating your communications environment, and it will lead you through your first on-line connection. But if this book is the key, it is also the map. In fact, much of the latter half of this book is dedicated to showing you just what you can do once you connect. It will direct you to on-line points of interest no matter what your interests may be, and introduce you to new things that you can find no where else but on line.

This book, as a key and as a map, is the beginning of a great adventure. It was written for people who are ready to make their first on-line expedition, no matter what their experience with computers. This book is for people who are considering the purchase of a modem, but aren't sure what they can do with one. It's for people who just bought a modem and are eager to put it to use. It is for people who got a computer with a modem already installed and are wondering what to do with it. It's for people who have had a modem for a very long time, but have never really exploited its capabilities. If you are new to communications, this book will tell you everything you need to know to get up and running. If you're a whiz at communications, this book is a refresher of basic principles and an opportunity to explore new avenues in on-line connections.

This book is *not* a techie manual full of communications jargon or all the other techno mumble jumble that has led so many people for so long to think that connecting is so hard. You won't find dense chapters defining the inner workings of communications protocols, international standards, or telecommunications networks. What you will find is the information you need— at exactly the level you need to know it—to connect your computer with other computers, so you can be more productive, better informed, and have more than a little fun along the way.

HOW THIS BOOK WORKS

I hope this book needs no explanation, yet there are four things important to note: pictures, symbols, sidebars, and keyword boxes. First, and most obviously, this book is full of wonderful pictures. Without them, this book would not be nearly as helpful as I hope it is. These rich illustrations show how things look. More importantly, they explain how things work. Most of all, they bring the context of everyday images to the words that accompany them.

Secondly, for most purposes, communications is communications no matter what type of computer—PC-compatible, Macintosh, and so on—you use. In general, the term "PC" is an acronym for personal computers—both IBM compatibles and Macs. There are, however, a few instances where procedures, hardware, or software may differ depending on the computer you use. And there are some on-line services that specialize in particular computer systems. In these cases, the book uses symbols to differentiate computer-specific information. **PC** represents PC-specific information and **MAC** signifies Macintosh-specific information.

This book avoids digging unnecessarily into technical detail when what you really want to know is *how to connect*. From time to time, however, technical information and occasional digressions are insightful and perhaps even interesting. That's why this book uses sidebars. These short sections are separate from the main text, but provide insights and information that you may also want to know.

KEYWORD BOXES

To help you access resources on the various services, you'll find keyword boxes in Chapters 11 and 12. They look like this:

ZiffNet	Resource	Go Word
	After Hours forum	AFTERHOURS
	Software games	PBSARC

That's all you need to know to use this book. I'm looking forward to seeing you on line soon.

CompuServe: 76000,17

America Online: SHIPLEY

Prodigy: RGGT63A

MCI Mail: CSHIPLEY

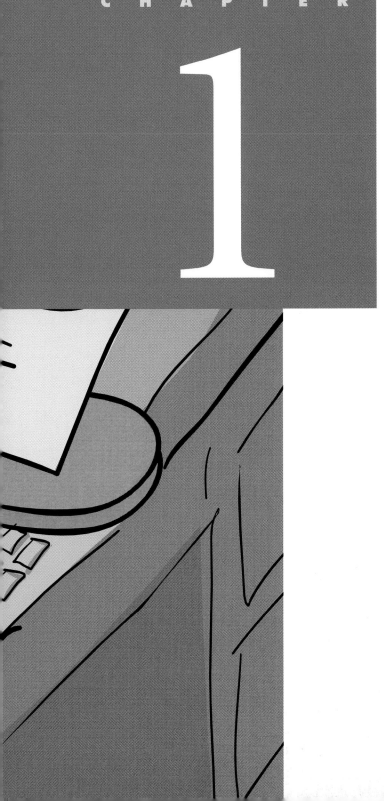

WORLDS OF POSSIBILITIES

Connecting. The idea seems simple enough. People linking their computers to other computers in order to communicate with one another. They exchange information, share data, and talk about ideas. But just what kind of information do they exchange? What data can they share? Just what do they talk about?

You might be surprised. Your personal computer, modem, and communications software open worlds of possibilities: libraries of information, shopping opportunities of all kinds, personal financial services, travel information, games, sports, weather, and much, much more—all available at the other end of the phone line.

WHO'S OUT THERE?

So what exactly does on line mean? *On line* is any place that computer users go via modems and telephone lines to meet with one another. On line can be a commercial service, such as CompuServe, Prodigy, or America Online, where many members connect to a central system to gather information and exchange ideas. On line can be a local bulletin board system—a single computer into which users call to read messages or copy software programs to their computers at home or work. On line can be an electronic mail service, such as MCI Mail or AT&T Mail, that individuals use to send messages to other service users. (You'll learn much more about all these specific kinds of on-line connections in later chapters. For now, just open your mind to all the wonderful possibilities that are available when you use a modem to connect to another computer.) Sometimes, the terms going on line and connecting are used interchangeably because both refer to essentially the same thing: any kind of electronic connection between computers.

Who goes on line? Literally millions of people just like you. On-line services and bulletin board systems are virtual cities teeming with activity. The same people you might meet on a city street can be found on line talking about the same things they talk about on street corners. And the errands they do at the post office, the bank, the local shops, the newsstand, and the library—they're doing them on line, too.

There are computer enthusiasts talking about the latest technologies, copying software programs from the on-line network to their own PCs, and swapping war stories about hardware upgrades. And there are lawyers, too, checking into electronic law libraries to find legal rulings that support their cases. There are investors buying and selling stocks, business travelers rearranging airline tickets, and collectors bartering everything from vintage baseball cards to antique automobiles.

Children talk with other kids about homework, fads, television, and music. They compete with one another in electronic games. They find information for school projects, and, more often than not, they learn something new.

Shoppers come on line to get the skinny on what car dealers really pay for a particular car. They scan electronic databases to find out who's offering the best price on the laser printer of their choice. Sometimes they just get snagged by a really great deal and buy products—while they're on line.

There are whole communities of fence-post chatters talking about politics, sports, current affairs, and the arts. If you have an interest, a social cause, or a point of view, there's someone on line ready to talk to you. In fact, every day people are meeting one another and making new friends. And every once in a while, couples fall in love, meet, and get married.

ALL THE NEWS

If you're a news junkie, on line is the place for up-to-the-minute information. The Associated Press provides hourly news updates through CompuServe and other on-line services. The *San Jose Mercury News* and *The Chicago Tribune* post each morning's edition on America Online. But on-line services don't just wait for news to come across the "wire." They keep on top of the latest stories themselves. During the 1992 presidential election, for example, Prodigy updated voter tallies as each state reported its results. Services also poll members and report the ebb and flow of popular opinion on a variety of news issues.

A WORLD OF CONNECTIONS

A whole new world packed with news, conversation, and
information opens up when you go on line.

Of course, there's much more than front-page news on on-line services. You can
get weather reports for any location across the country or around the world—including
satellite and radar maps. Sports fans tune into on-line services to gather the scores from
all the games, get the scoop on who's been traded where, and find out who's on and off
the injured reserve list. Hollywood watchers get the low-down on all the entertainment
news, from the latest television deals to movie reviews and soap opera summaries. From
time to time, the stars even come out on-line to talk to their fans.

REFERENCE DESK

Have you ever wondered about… anything? Well, you can probably find the answer
on line. When was the Magna Carta signed? How fast does the bullet train go? How
many movies did Charlie Chaplin make? What should I pay for a new Ford Taurus? What

can I do to treat poison ivy? Should we send our child to Princeton? And where will we get the money to pay for it?

If you can imagine a question, there is an on-line source to answer it. Most popular reference works—and many obscure ones—are now available in electronic form, enabling you to dial in, search a database, and get the information you need. There are dozens of databases that have abstracts and full articles from literally hundreds of thousands of magazines, journals, and newsletters. Government information—from census data to agency regulations—is all available on line. You can check government tax regulations (do you have to pay social security taxes for your nanny?), research the demographic profiles of cities and towns across the country (where's the best place to locate a new frozen yogurt factory?), and stay current on pending government contracts (maybe your paving business can bid on that new highway job).

Consumer Reports, Books in Print, Marquis Who's Who, Magill's Survey of Cinema, Peterson's College Database, a half-dozen encyclopedias, dictionaries, and thesauruses, even phone books—you can use them all on line.

MONEY MATTERS

It's hard to be a smart investor these days without going on line. In fact, most personal finance and investment software have built-in links to on-line services. There's no need to wait for the morning paper to find out how your stock did in the day's market. On line, you can get instant stock price quotes throughout the trading day. Thinking about investing in a new company? On-line services provide the latest news from Dow Jones, financial and company reports, ratings from Standard & Poors, and much more to help you make wise investment decisions. When you're ready to put your money into the company, you can buy the stock on line, too. A number of brokerage firms, including Quick & Reilly, Dreyfus, Fidelity Investments, and Charles Schwabb, make their services available electronically.

ON-LINE MONEY MANAGEMENT

Paying bills electonically makes quick work of financial chores.

1 Using your computer, tell the electronic bill-paying service that you want to pay the electric company.

2 The bill-paying service processes your transaction.

3 Funds from your bank account are transferred.

4 Your creditor's bank account receives the transferred funds.

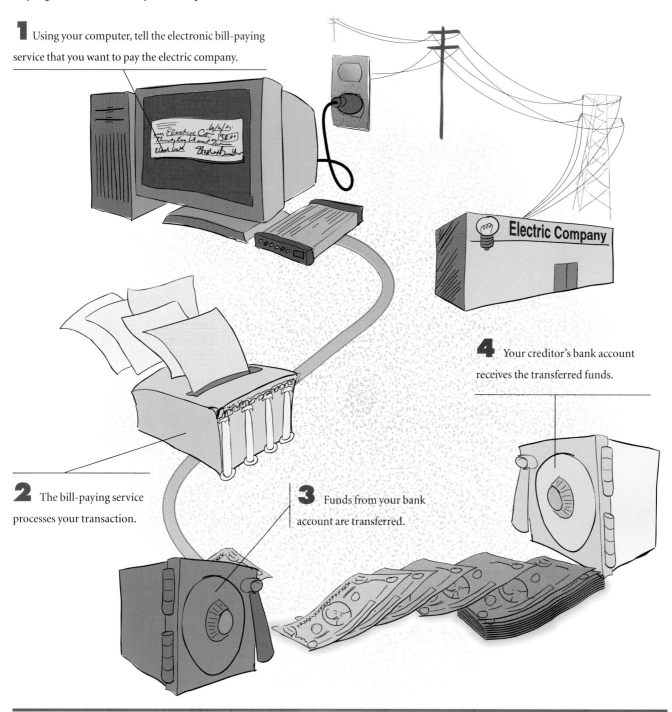

Popular personal finance programs, including Managing Your Money and Quicken, let you dial into on-line services and update your stock portfolio automatically. Another program, Fidelity Online Express, lets you buy and sell mutual funds through the Fidelity discount brokerage network. Reality Technology's innovative Smart Investor software and service gives all the tools investors need to evaluate, buy, track, and sell investments—all on line.

If you only dream about making your million in the stock market, on-line services let you make a game of it. CompuServe, for example, lets members compete with one another as they build imaginary portfolios. The player who makes the most money wins.

But on-line money management isn't just about investing. Some banks, such as Citibank in New York, let you handle basic bank transactions by dialing into the bank's computer and accessing your account. And a variety of services let you pay bills without ever writing a check. You simply send an electronic payment notice to the Checkfree or BillPay USA services, for example, and they transfer money from your account to pay the bills you specify—from major credit cards to the local drugstore.

THE ELECTRONIC MALL

Imagine if every mail order catalog in existence arrived on your doorstep. That's just about what it's like to shop on line. Brooks Brothers, Lands' End, JC Penney, Books On Tape, Barnes & Noble, Columbia House music club, Hammacher Schlemmer, JDR Microdevices, Omaha Steaks, the Metropolitan Museum of Art—these are just a sampling of the organizations selling their wares on line. Need to send flowers, a fruit basket, or maybe some specialty coffees or foods? Dozens of companies ready to serve you are just a modem connection away.

Although there are plenty of things to buy on line, there are also ways to be smarter about what you buy. *Consumer Reports*, for example, provides its product-test results electronically. You can find out how much you should spend on a new car, including dealer prices for every option and tips on negotiating the deal. If you're in the market for computer products, Ziff Buyer's Market and PC Catalog are two services that provide a complete listing of direct marketing sources for hardware and software. In seconds, you can find out who's got the best price on hundreds of products. And the Boston Computer Exchange links buyers and sellers of used computer equipment.

If your idea of shopping is a lazy Saturday afternoon cruising yard sales, you'll find something on line, too. On-line classifieds are a giant swap meet where you can buy or sell just about anything—without ever taking the car out of the garage.

TRAVEL AND LEISURE

Planning a trip? Make an on-line service the first stop on your itinerary. From airline tickets to hotel reservations, you can handle all your travel arrangements yourself, without having to "hold for the next available agent." You can book flights, reserve rental cars, even sign up for an exotic cruise. Many prominent travel services are available to on-line users, but one of the most useful is the EAASY SABRE reservation system that enables you to search for, compare, book, and purchase airline tickets, reserve rental cars, and schedule hotel accommodations. You'll also find other handy traveler's resources, including the Official Airline Guide Electonic Travel Services, which features up-to-date listings of more than 200,000 flights and a bevy of travel-related information, including frequent-flier program rules, toll-free airline, hotel, and car rental phone numbers, and much more.

You might expect to find Zagat's Restaurant Survey on line—and you will. And you likely won't be surprised to find recommendations from other on-line users on the best bed-and-breakfasts, out-of-the-way restaurants, interesting sites, and all the rest. But you might be surprised to learn that U.S. State Department travel and visa advisories are on line and updated as international situations change.

THE MAIL'S HERE

It won't be surprising if the twenty-nine cent stamp winds up on the endangered species list. More and more people are taking advantage of fast, immediate electronic mail to get their messages across. Anyone who signs up for a major on-line service automatically gets a "mailbox" to receive electronic mail, commonly referred to as e-mail. There are even services, such as MCI Mail and AT&T mail, that do nothing but act as an electronic post office, delivering e-mail to their members.

An electronic message costs about the same to send as a paper letter, but with added benefits. You can be sure that your message is instantly delivered to the recipient's electronic mailbox. You can even request a "return receipt" that notifies you when the recipient has opened your message. If you need to send a mass-mailing, you can write one message and send it to dozens of mailboxes, without copying and addressing all those envelopes. And when you want to reply to a message, the system automatically addresses the envelope; you just fill in your response.

E-mail is a great way for friends and family to stay in touch, too. One message, sent to every family member, for example, can launch a discussion of the type usually shared around the Thanksgiving table. And e-mail lets you quickly speak what's on your mind. Do you have a gripe for the president? Drop him an electronic message. In fact, according to one news report, the White House gets up to 5,000 e-mail messages a week.

ENTERTAINMENT

Just because you are home alone doesn't mean you have to play by yourself. Imagine, instead, going into combat, descending a dark cave, or rocketing into space—by dialing into an on-line service to match wits with other members in on-line interactive games. GEnie provides a host of multiplayer games. Prodigy's Baseball Manager is a season-long venture that pits you against other members in a rotisserie baseball league. Rotisserie baseball uses the performance of real-life baseball players across the major leagues to

HOW TO BE A SMART CONSUMER

On-line services are a fantastic resource for car shoppers. You can comparison shop by scanning reviews, get the lowdown on dealer prices, and even ask other on-line users for advice on making a deal for your new wheels.

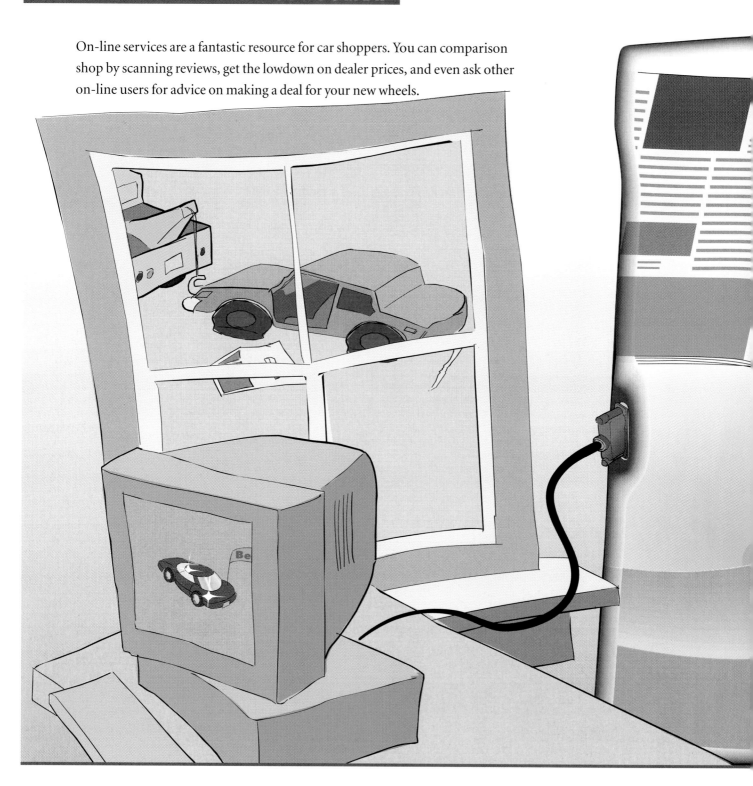

Ultimate CAR

Best Buy

DEALER INVOICE

	Dealer Price	Suggest Retail
Base Price	11,840	13,261
Air Conditioning	664	744
Floor Mats	52	58
Limited Slip Dif.	200	224
California Emissions	70	78
Package A	1,096	1,228
Total Options	2,068	2,316
Total Veh. & Opt.	15,990	17,909

...sponse to your inquiry about ...ur upcoming car purchase — I have just such a car, and I can highly recommend it. When I bought mine I checked it out here on the net and determined that it was just the car for me. I've had mine for ten months and love it. Oh, be sure to get the limited slip differential—I've found it invaluable ;-) Ginny

ELECTRONIC MAIL

Electronic mail is a great way to stay in touch with people around the world. Messages zip from user to user in an instant. And the mail system will even tell you when your message has been read by sending you a return receipt.

chart the performance of the game-player's dream team. You draft and trade players, arrange the lineups, and play games with other on-line league members. How your team performs in a given game depends on how the real-life ball players did in that night's outing at the ballpark. Just about every on-line service hosts lots of games, including trivia contests of every flavor and stripe with chances to win real prizes.

On-line services offer a host of downloadable games, too. You can copy these game programs from the on-line service to your own computer and play them after you've disconnected from the on-line service. Games are among the most frequently downloaded programs, and you can find them in a number of categories including sports, arcades, education, role playing, strategy, and many more.

But games aren't the only entertainment you'll find on line. Many on-line services have complete movie, theatre, book, and arts reviews to let you know what entertainment is worth your pursuit and what isn't. On-line service users get together in special discussion areas to share the opinions on the latest in pop culture. And oftentimes authors, television actors, and movie stars come on line to talk with their fans.

SOFTWARE AVAILABILITY

Picture a room filled with floppy disks. There are word processing and spreadsheet programs. There are programs that teach kids to read and spell and multiply and subtract. And there are drawing programs and desktop publishing packages, and thousands of ready-made graphics to use with them. In one corner of the room there's nothing but utilities to back up your hard drive, fine-tune your system, and make your PC easier and more fun to use. There's a stack of programs that make music, and mountains of databases to manage everything from business client lists to baseball card collections. The middle of the room is piled high with games, games, and more games.

You'll need a very large imagination to picture just how big this room needs to be to hold all the software available at the other end of a modem connection. Most of the programs are *shareware*, which you can copy to your PC and try before paying for them. Others are absolutely free. And they're all just a phone call away.

THE "VIRTUAL COMMUNITY"

You're never lonely when you're on line; there are always lots of people to talk to, and talk to, and talk to. But what is everyone talking about? Food, politics, religion, fitness, literature, hobbies, art, music, their pets, and their pet peeves.

On-line services are "virtual communities" where people come together to share ideas, tell their secrets, and criticize and compliment just about everything. In computer speak, "virtual" is any electronic experience that mimics real life. You may have heard the term "virtual reality" used to describe computer-simulated experiences that seem to the user to be like the real thing. A *virtual community* is a group of people who come together and interact, even though they come from across the country or around the globe.

SOFTWARE AT YOUR FINGERTIPS

You'll have to stretch your imagination to envision a library big
enough to hold all the software available to you on line.

On-line services, then, become a forum for meeting people who share your interests and ideas. No matter what your profession or passion, there's a group already talking about it. You can talk about fly-fishing with someone in Wisconsin, even though you live in Alabama. Or you can share your recipe for barbecue sauce with a "neighbor" in Maine. No matter that you live in Texas. Because when you're on line, location doesn't matter; you're still all in the same "place."

Catching the latest news, doing your banking, shopping, playing games, talking to people around the globe—it all sounds great, but isn't it *expensive?* The honest answer is yes and no. Connections do cost money. Even local bulletin board services must pay for the hardware and software, and perhaps even personnel, to keep the service up and running. Larger on-line services must keep a network of larger computers up and running day in and day out so that you can dial in to get the information you want, when you want it. They buy the rights to make information such as encyclopedias, news, sports scores, stock quotes, weather reports, airline schedules, and much more available to their members on line. They need a staff of programmers to keep the computers running and editors to make sure you always get the most current information. And their biggest costs, by far, are telecommunications costs that enable you to make a local call to access their services, even when their service is located across the country.

Ultimately, you help pay for these costs. Depending on what you are connecting to, the costs will vary. Sometimes, the charge is as little as a local phone call to a bulletin board service that you can use as much as you'd like at no additional costs. Other times, the bulletin board operator will ask you to pay a small registration fee to support the on-going operation of the board. Most on-line services charge a membership fee—typically less than $10 a month—that gives you access to many, if not all, the service's features.

In addition to this membership fee, you may be charged for the amount of time you use all or some parts of the service. These charges, often referred to as *connect time rates*, typically range from about $4 per hour to as much as $20 or more, often depending on

A VIRTUAL COMMUNITY

People from around the world can talk with one another as though they were neighbors by getting together on line.

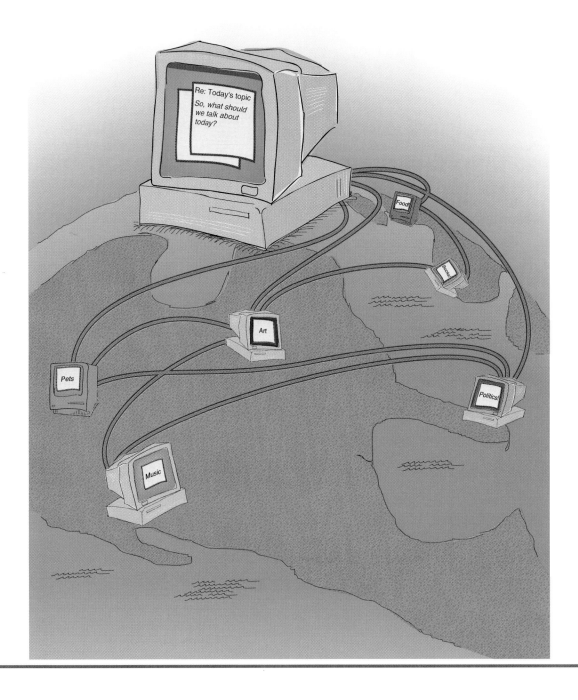

what time of day you call the service and what modem speed you use. The theory here is that it is cheaper for on-line services to cover their telecommunications costs during nonpeak evening and weekend hours. Faster modems allow members to get much more information in a shorter time on line, so you pay a premium for that extra information. Incidentally, because you can get so much more information sent to your computer using a faster modem, it ultimately costs less to use a faster modem, even if you pay a bit more for the connect time because you are connected to the service for significantly fewer minutes.

Most on-line services have special service plans that include several hours of connect time in the monthly membership fee. As a result, you can get a lot of use from a service such as America Online or Prodigy for less than $10 a month.

2

If you've ever traveled in foreign countries, you know that customs vary greatly from place to place. On-line communications is a world all its own, and it, too, has its own set of customs and courtesies. Just as it is important to know the local customs when you travel, knowing the etiquette of on-line communications will make you a more welcome member of the on-line community.

A LANGUAGE ALL ITS OWN

Perhaps the first word in good manners is to learn the few key words and phrases that will help you understand your new environment and get along better with the people in the on-line community. On-line communications has a language all its own. There are dozens of technical terms—baud, parity, protocol, and handshake, for example—that you may hear from time to time. Throughout this book, I'll define those terms in context. Rest assured, though, that you'll not have to develop a whole new "techie" vocabulary in order to gain all the advantages of on-line communications.

But there's much more to on-line language than dull communications jargon. The on-line community has its own unique conversational words and phrases, and these are the words you'll really want to know. Furthermore, each on-line environment has its own dialect. For example, conversations might be called messages, notes, or threads, depending on the service you are using. But there are a number of words and phrases that are constant across all services. Here are a few that you'll need to know to be part of the "in" on-line crowd.

> ▶ *bulletin board system* also *BBS* n: *an on-line electronic service on which users can exchange messages and data or program files, most often for public consumption by all other members. Some services, such as Prodigy, refer to the places where members write messages to one another as* bulletin boards.

▶ *chat* n: *an on-line dialog in which two or more people participate in live electronic conversation, also known as a* conference *or* CB. v: *the act of participating in a live electronic conversation.*

▶ *download* v: *the act of copying a file from a bulletin board or on-line service to your PC.* n: *an electronic file that has been copied from a bulletin board or on-line service to your PC. Also referred to as* DL, *usually in the text of an on-line message.*

▶ *electronic mail* also *e-mail* n: *a private message sent from one person to another via an on-line information network.* v: *to send a message.*

▶ *flame* n: *a message or group of messages that are hostile, angry, or outrageous (did you see that* flame *about Microsoft's new support policies?).* v: *to post a disparaging or controversial message.* *flamer* n: *one who regularly posts angry messages.*

▶ *forum* n: *originally from CompuServe, an area on an on-line service devoted to a single topic (the politics* forum*).*

▶ *forward* v: *to pass along to someone else an electronic mail message previously sent to you.*

▶ *log on* v: *to connect to an on-line service by dialing the service and entering name and password.*

▶ *lurker* n: *one who reads and "listens in" on discussions without participating or contributing in the discussion.* *lurk* v: *the act of reading messages without posting responses.*

▶ *on-line service* n: *a commercial venture that provides information via an electronic connection (for example, America Online, CompuServe, Delphi, GEnie, Prodigy).*

▶ *post* v: *to place a message on a bulletin board or in a forum for public reading.*

▶ *sysop* n: *a person who monitors on-line conversations to be sure they stay on track and aboveboard. Some services refer to this person as the* board manager *or* guide.

▶ *thread* n: *a series of messages or conversations that follow a single thought or topic; one continuous discussion.*

▶ *upload* v: *to send a file from your PC to a bulletin board or on-line service.* n: *the file that has been sent to the service.*

With this list, you're well on your way to developing a whole new vocabulary. You'll learn several other new words as you make your way through this book, and even more as you explore on-line services. In fact, many terms will be specific to the on-line services you choose to use. As you come across new words or familiar words used in strange new ways, it is absolutely okay to ask other on-line service users just what they mean. Remember, they were new to on-line services once, too.

MINDING YOUR MANNERS ON LINE

For all its advantages, on-line communications have one very major drawback: They're totally dependent on the words you type to communicate your meaning. The gestures, eye movements, intonation, volume, smiles, and grimaces that help people understand the meaning and innuendo of your spoken communication are absent from your on-line messages. The on-line community has developed its own code to add this subtle layer of meaning to on-line messages. In polite on-line conversation, for example, you use upper- and lowercase characters, just as you would in a business letter or office memo. The mix of upper- and lowercase is easier to read online. But how do you raise your voice in an on-line message? Simple: TYPE IN ALL CAPS! The recipient will know you're yelling. But never type in all capital letters unless you really do want to yell out your point. Messages in all capital letters are very hard to read and considered quite rude in on-line circles.

ADDING EMPHASIS TO WORDS AND PHRASES

And what if you want to add emphasis to just a word or phrase, but you don't exactly want to yell it? On-line messaging doesn't support italic or bold text. Place an asterisk at either end of the word for *just the right* emphasis.

Perhaps the most important courtesy is KISS: Keep it short and simple. On most on-line services, brevity is not only the soul of wit, but also the key to more effective communications and lower connect time costs. When you write a letter to a friend on paper, you have the whole page to convey your ideas. With just one glance, your friend can take in the scope of your message, easily skip to the middle or end, and very quickly grasp the essence of your words. Not so on line. When you write an electronic message, you have a few lines transmitted one screen at a time. The recipient of your message must read your message sequentially—there's no skipping to the end to find key ideas buried there. As the communicator, you need to make your point quickly. Otherwise, your on-line pen pal may give up on your message before you've had your say. That's why short and sweet is the rule of thumb on line. Try to keep your messages to one or two screens. "Four score and seven years ago, our forefathers brought forth upon this continent a new nation" may sound good in a speech and it may read well on paper, but on line, "This country was founded 87 yrs. ago" plays much better.

To help keep messages brief, the on-line community has come up with hundreds, perhaps thousands, of shortcuts to say in a few letters what would otherwise take a dozen or more characters. The point of these acronyms is to make on-line messages brief, using the fewest characters to communicate the most information. Many of these acronyms will already be familiar to you; they are commonly used in everyday communications—ASAP (as soon as possible) and FYI (for your information). Many acronyms are specific to certain situations. The military, for example, has its own abbreviations, such as SNAFU (situation normal, all "fouled" up). Star Trek fans have theirs: SFS (search for Spock) and TFF (the final frontier). As you participate in bulletin board discussions, you'll come to learn the acronyms unique to various special interests. And just as when you encounter unfamiliar new terms, when you don't know the meaning of an acronym, just ask.

COMMUNICATING WITH TLAS

Roughly translated, the message reads:

Great! Gee, I wish I said that. I'm rolling on the floor laughing! You're right on the money. There ain't no such thing as a free lunch. Thank you very much for the insight.

Ta ta for now,
George

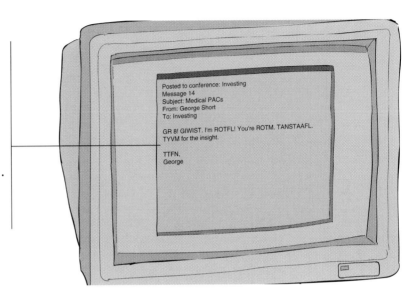

Posted to conference: Investing
Message 14
Subject: Medical PACs
From: George Short
To: Investing

GR 8! GIWIST. I'm ROTFL! You're ROTM. TANSTAAFL. TYVM for the insight.

TTFN.
George

These shortened messages could fill an entire dictionary. Let's get started with a few dozen of the most frequently used TLAs (three letter acronyms). IMHO (in my humble opinion), the list covers the acronyms you're most likely to see on line. BTW (by the way), the creative uses of many TLAs will have you LOL (laughing out loud). You'll notice that many TLAs have grown beyond three letters. TLA generally includes acronyms of any length, but in the interest of precision, some on-line users have adopted MLA to refer to multiletter acronyms. See the figure A TLA Dictionary for more examples of TLAs.

In addition to cryptic TLAs that pepper electronic conversations, on-line communicators have dozens of phonetic contractions, or words that are spelled like they sound. Many of these contractions, such as "tho," and "thru," are standard fare. Others are a bit more creative. For example, you may be asked, "how RU," and you could answer, "fine, thx." So if you see a strange letter combination and you aren't sure what it might mean,

A TLA DICTIONARY

10Q—thank you

$0.02—throwing your two cents in

A

AAMOF—as a matter of fact

ADN—any day now

AFAIK—as far as I know

ATSL—along the same line

AWGTHTGTTA—are we going to have to go through this again?

AWHFY—are we having fun yet?

B

B4—before

BAC—by any chance

BAG(L)—busting a gut (laughing)

BBFN—bye bye for now; *also*

B4N—bye for now

BCNU—be seeing you

BION—believe it or not

BRB—be right back (used when you leave an on-line conference so that others know not to address messages to you while you are away)

BTA—but then again

BTW—by the way; *also* **OBTW**— oh, by the way

BTSOOM—beats the "stuffing" out of me

BWG—big wide grin; *also* **DLG**— devilish little grin, **GLG**—goofy little grin

BYKT(A)—but you knew that (already)

C

CMIIW—correct me if I'm wrong

CU L8R—see you later; *also* **CU**—see you

CYA—cover your a___

D

DL—download

DQOTD—dumb question of the day

E

EMFBI—excuse me for butting in

EOD—end of discussion

EOL—end of lecture

ESOSL—endless snorts of stupid laughter

F

FITB—fill in the blank

FUBAR—fouled up beyond all recognition

FUD—fear, uncertainty, and doubt

FWIW—for what it's worth

FYI—for your information

G

GD&R—grin, duck & run (used when you've made a wisecrack or friendly insult)

GIGO—garbage in, garbage out

GIWIST—gee I wish I'd said that

GMTA—great minds think alike

GOK—God only knows

GOWI—get on with it

GR8—great

I

IAC—in any case; *also* **IAE**—in any event

IANAL—I am not a lawyer; *also* **IANAD**—I am not a doctor, as well as other variations

ICOCBW—I could, of course, be wrong

IMO—in my opinion (used to designate a point of view that often isn't as humble as it is billed); *also* **IMHO**—in my humble opinion, **IMNSHO**—in my not so humble opinion, **IMCO**—in my considered opinion, **IMCDO**—in my conceited, dogmatic opinion

IMV—in my view

IOW—in other words

ITFA—in the final analysis

ITSFWI—if the shoe fits, wear it

J

JOOC—just out of curiosity

K

KHYF—know how you feel

L

L8R—later

LOL—laughing out loud; *also*

LA—laughing aloud, **LTMSH**
—laughing 'til my sides hurt

M

MLA—multiletter acronym; *also*

TLA—three-letter acronym

MYOB—mind your own
business

N

NAVY—never again
volunteer yourself

NICBDAT—nothing
is certain but
death and taxes

NIMBY—not in my backyard

NRN—no reply necessary

NTIM—not that it matters

NTYMI—now that you
mention it

O

OAS—on another subject

OIC—oh, I see

OTL—out to lunch

OTOH—on the other hand

P

PMJI—pardon my jumping in

(used when joining a conference
or chat or when you want to add
your opinion to a discussion)

PITA—pain in the "anatomy"

R

ROFL—rolling on floor laughing;
also **ROFAHMSL**—rolling on floor
and holding my sides laughing,

ROTFL—rolling on the floor
laughing, **ROFLASTC** (or
ROFLASC)—rolling on floor
laughing and scaring the cat,

FDROTFL—falling down rolling
on the floor laughing,

FOTCL—falling off the chair
laughing

ROTBA—reality on the blink
again

ROTM—right on the money

RSN—real soon now (used
cynically, to describe when
you might get around to doing
something)

S

SITD—still in the dark

SOW—speaking of which

SWAG—simple wild a__ guess

T

TAF—that's all, folks!

TAFN—that's all for now

TANSTAAFL—there ain't no such
thing as a free lunch

TBYB—try before you buy

TIA—thanks in advance

TIC—tongue in cheek

TLA—three-letter acronym; *also*

MLA—multiletter acronym

TOBAL—there oughta be a law

TTBOMK—to the best of my
knowledge

TTFN—ta ta for now

TTYL(A)—talk (type) to you
later (alligator)

TYVM—thank you very much

W

WOA—work of art

WYGIWYPF—what you get is what
you pay for

WYSIWYG—what you see is what
you get

WYTYSYDG—what you thought you
saw, you didn't get

Y

YASQ—yet another stupid
question

YGLT—you're gonna love this

YMBK—you must be kidding; *also*

YMBJ—you must be joking

YMMV—your mileage may vary

fall back on the advice of our grade school teachers: sound it out. You may just find that you *do* know what's being said.

WHAT'S AN EMOTICON?

For many on-line communicators, simple bracketed comments just aren't expressive enough. They needed something else to convey the spirit in which messages were intended. So these folks came up with whole galleries full of *emoticons*, strings of type characters that say what they mean. The most simple emoticon is the smiley :) composed of a colon and a closed parenthesis. The smiley gave way to the frown :(and then dozens and dozens of variations started rolling in. Today there are hundreds of symbols to communicate a wide range of emotions.

When you see one of these character strings on line, the best way to make sense of it is to tilt your head to the left and look at it sideways. If you observe a colon, a hyphen, and an end parenthesis, you'll be face to face with the standard smiley. See for yourself:

The use of an emoticon may also depend on the context. A message using :-# means "I wear braces" in a discussion about dental work, but means "I'm censoring my remarks" in a discussion about the performance of your employer.

COMMUNICATING GESTURES

Acronyms make messages short and sweet, but on-line users often need to show their gestures, too. Members of the on-line community have come up with a variety of ways to express "body language" in words. Many of these are simple bracketed comments, such as <grin> or <g> to designate a smile or suggest that a comment is made in jest. If you're making a really big joke, let your on-line friends know by using <gg> or <BG>. If you are embarrassed, you may need to <blush>, and a coy <wink> can often keep you out of trouble. So can an <ahem> to clear your throat after you make a smart remark. Other "gestures" include a <shrug>, a <smirk>, and even a heavy <sigh>.

EMOTICONS

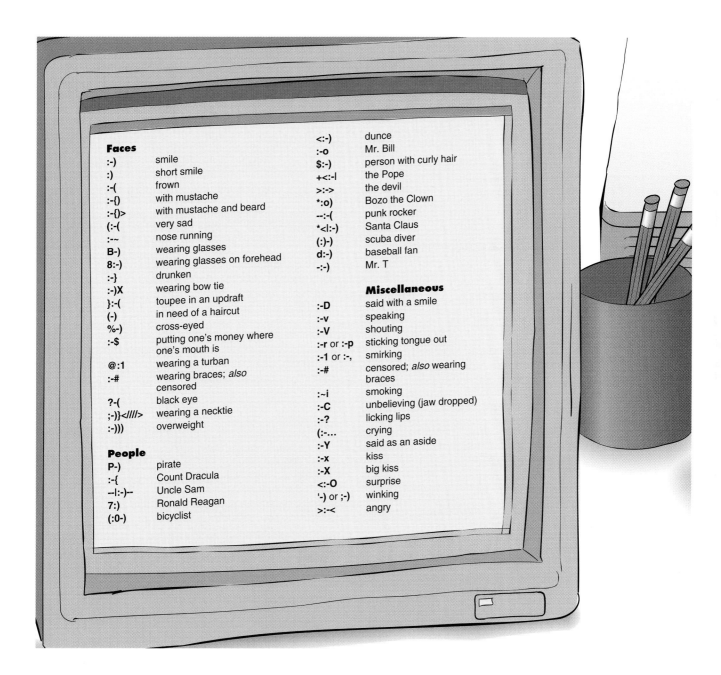

Faces

:-)	smile
:)	short smile
:-(	frown
:-{}	with mustache
:-{}>	with mustache and beard
(:-(	very sad
:-~	nose running
B-)	wearing glasses
8:-)	wearing glasses on forehead
:-}	drunken
:-)X	wearing bow tie
}:-(	toupee in an updraft
(-)	in need of a haircut
%-)	cross-eyed
:-$	putting one's money where one's mouth is
@:1	wearing a turban
:-#	wearing braces; *also* censored
?-(	black eye
;-)}</////>	wearing a necktie
:-)))	overweight

People

P-)	pirate
:-{	Count Dracula
--I:-)--	Uncle Sam
7:)	Ronald Reagan
(:0-)	bicyclist

<:-)	dunce
:-o	Mr. Bill
$:-)	person with curly hair
+<:-l	the Pope
>:->	the devil
*:o)	Bozo the Clown
--:-(	punk rocker
*<l:-)	Santa Claus
(:)-)	scuba diver
d:-)	baseball fan
-:-)	Mr. T

Miscellaneous

:-D	said with a smile
:-v	speaking
:-V	shouting
:-r or :-p	sticking tongue out
:-1 or :-,	smirking
:-#	censored; *also* wearing braces
:~i	smoking
:-C	unbelieving (jaw dropped)
:-?	licking lips
(:-...	crying
:-Y	said as an aside
:-x	kiss
:-X	big kiss
<:-O	surprise
'-) or ;-)	winking
>:-<	angry

You use emoticons just as you use gestures in a conversation. For example: My great, great Uncle Louie died. (:-... Then his lawyer called and told me I inherited a million bucks! :-D Not that I won't miss, Uncle Louie, of course :(

YOUR ON-LINE RIGHTS

All this talk of showing emotion begs the question of just how much emotion you can show. Just how far can you go on-line? Each on-line service has its own guidelines for good taste. Many are family-oriented services that prefer the Seven Dirty Words stay off their messaging systems. Other on-line services provide special adults-only forums to discuss issues such as human sexuality (in all its various forms). And there are many free-for-all bulletin boards where anything goes. To know what conversation topics are appropriate on the services you choose to use, check out the membership agreements carefully. These will outline exactly what goes and what doesn't.

If you do step out of line, unintentionally or otherwise, nearly all on-line services and bulletin boards retain the right to remove your message from public view. When this happens, a sysop generally informs you of your mistake and asks you to repost your note in more appropriate form. This practice has been perceived by some as censorship. To be sure, there are arguments on all sides of this question. Some people say that because members of on-line services agree to certain rules, it is reasonable for the services to scan messages for violations of the rules. Others believe that on-line services and bulletin boards violate a member's First Amendment rights when any message is removed from public view. Tangled up in these arguments are the on-line service's legal liabilities. Is the service responsible if one member slanders another in an on-line message? If members use the service to publicly conduct illegal business, is the service an accomplice to the crime? Can a service be subpoenaed to turn over records of on-line conversations to the courts? Lawyers and judges are wrangling over these issues and have yet to come up with complete answers.

One thing does seem to be clear: Personal electronic messages sent and received on public electronic mail and on-line services are private, much like paper mail sent through the U.S. Postal Service is private. On-line services, contrary to rumors that flare up from time to time, aren't reading the contents of members' messages. Within the confines of electronic mail, you can say to anyone else anything you want. These messages are for your eyes and those of your recipient only.

3

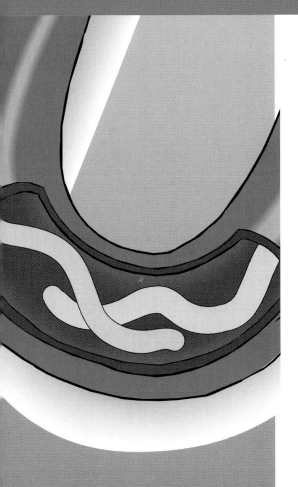

WHAT YOU SHOULD KNOW ABOUT VIRUSES

What is a Computer Virus?

▪

Virus Detection

▪

Virus Prevention

▪

Myths and Truths about Viruses

In the minds of many personal computer users, connecting to bulletin-board and on-line services carries with it a risk they'd rather not take—the risk of contracting a computer virus. These so called viruses infect personal computers and destroy data. Oddly enough, the risk of getting a virus through an on-line connection is relatively slim and virtually nonexistent if you know how to protect yourself. But like many fears, the fear of catching a computer virus through an on-line connection in large measure grew out of one infamous situation.

In March 1992, Michelangelo was on the minds of every personal computer user. Not Michelangelo the Italian sculptor. Michelangelo the rogue computer virus. According to well-documented rumors, a destructive computer program would self-activate on March 6, the birthday of the artist Michelangelo, and destroy any data residing on the PC on which it was running.

Unlike any other event to hit personal computing, the Michelangelo virus made the local evening news, the national evening news, and even some syndicated news magazines and talk shows. Like citizens moving to higher ground because of reports of an impending flood, PC users prepared their computers against this potential danger. By March 5, many computer users had invested in and put to use antivirus software to ferret out and destroy this and other potentially dangerous programs. Other users backed up their hard-disks, enabling them to recover important data should the Michelangelo virus strike their computers. Still others just shut down their PCs until the scare had passed.

This preparation paid off. By even the most exaggerated estimates, fewer than 20,000 computers were affected by Michelangelo—less than one-tenth of one percent of all PC users. Nevertheless, the Michelangelo virus served to put all computer users on warning. PC users had heard reports of exotic-sounding viruses—Jerusalem, Columbus Day, Stoned, Falling Letters, Murphy, Ping Pong, and thousands of others. PC users were vaguely aware of the potential danger of these out-of-control programs, but, until Michelangelo, most computer users thought viruses were something that happened to other PCs, not to their own.

NOTE *The Jerusalem Virus was one of the first known viruses. It was discovered in 1988 at Hebrew University in Israel. The program was designed to activate on Friday, May 13, 1988. Today, there are many strains of this virus, and literally thousands of other viruses.*

While it's not vital that you understand the intricacies of viruses, it's good to know how they work, how to tell if you have one, and what you can do to cure them, should your computer be infected. Better yet, you need to know how to keep your computer from getting infected in the first place.

WHAT IS A COMPUTER VIRUS?

A computer virus is simply a software program. But rather than performing some useful function, say, word processing, communications, or accounting, a virus is designed to perform some operation without your knowledge or authorization. Viruses can be relatively harmless practical jokes. They may consume some hard-disk storage space, rearrange text characters, or flash a silly message on your screen, for example, but otherwise do no real damage to your system. Many viruses, however, are extremely destructive. The well-known Datacrime virus, for example, launches a low-level format of your hard disk, wiping out any shred of data once stored there.

Typically, viruses are self-propagating. They infect a program by embedding themselves in it. When the program is activated, the virus copies itself and goes on to infect other programs on the system. More scurrilous viruses transfer themselves from the program to the hard disk's partition table, file allocation table, or boot sector—the parts of the hard disk that identify how the hard disk is organized, where programs and data are stored, and how to start up your computer system. From this position, the virus is poised to do even greater damage to your data.

Viruses spread from one computer to another when programs are shared between computers. This sharing may happen by copying programs to floppy disks and then copying the floppy to another hard disk. And programs can be shared by sending them over telephone lines via modem. This is why an understanding of viruses and other infectious programs is so important for on-line communicators. You need to be very careful about *what* programs you copy electronically to your computer and *where* you copy them from.

Like a virus in a plant or animal, a computer virus needs a host system—the computer—to accommodate it. Just as a virus infects the host, typically without the knowledge of the host, a computer virus infects a computer without the user's knowledge. Once on the computer system, the virus will hide itself by attaching to program files, making the virus difficult to detect. Then it may copy itself, spread to other program files, and infect other systems to which those program files are copied. A virus can lie dormant on an infected computer until some external event—such as a date or time—triggers it. When that event occurs, the virus begins to exhibit itself. See the illustration How a Virus Infects a Computer System to get a better picture of how viruses go about their nasty business.

The following types of infectious programs each affect a computer in different ways:

▶ *Trojan Horses*   *In Greek mythology, a large wooden horse was left at the gates of the City of Troy. Thinking it a gift, the Trojans wheeled the horse into their city, closing the gates behind them. In the dark of night, Greek soldiers climbed out of the horse, opened the city gates to their fellow warriors, and conquered the City of Troy. Trojan Horse programs work much the same way on your computer. They appear to be perfectly useful programs, such as a game or a handy disk utility. In reality, they are dangerous programs lying in wait to do damage. When the presumably innocent program is run, the Trojan Horse becomes active and deletes files or otherwise makes data and programs on your hard disk inaccessible. The*

HOW A VIRUS INFECTS A COMPUTER SYSTEM

Viruses can enter your computer in three ways:

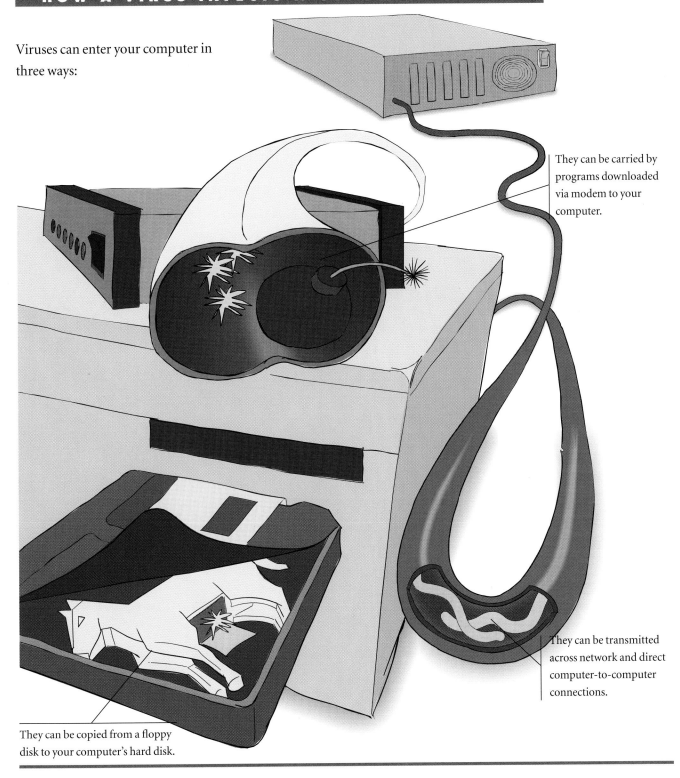

They can be carried by programs downloaded via modem to your computer.

They can be transmitted across network and direct computer-to-computer connections.

They can be copied from a floppy disk to your computer's hard disk.

chief difference between a Trojan Horse and a virus is that the Trojan Horse does not replicate itself. Instead, it does its damage when the disguised application is run. A "well-designed" Trojan Horse can secret its malicious behavior for long periods before the computer user ever discovers that something is wrong.

▶ *Worms   Unlike viruses and Trojan Horses, worms rarely do damage to data. Instead, they are tiny programs that replicate themselves over and over, filling up system memory (RAM) or hard-disk space. As the worm replicates, it causes the PC to operate more and more slowly as system resources are used to supply the worm, rather than the legitimate programs you are running. Worms can also be designed to wriggle their way through a computer network, for example, looking for specific information, such as passwords, and sending this information back to the worm's creator. Once the worm has accomplished its mission, it deletes itself, leaving no trace that it was ever there.*

▶ *Logic and Time Bombs   Much like a Trojan Horse, a logic or time bomb is a program that lies dormant until some predetermined set of conditions is met. A logic bomb is triggered by any number of circumstances, but might be set off, for example, when a particular DOS command is issued or a specific program is launched. A time bomb, as the name implies, goes off when the computer's system clock strikes a certain date or time. When these bombs go off, they can do any sort of damage, depending on what they were programmed to do. These bombs can be particularly difficult to eradicate because they can contaminate backed up data files, where they lie again, waiting to go off.*

Some viruses take on many of the attributes described above. For example, a Trojan Horse may destroy data files and infect other program files. Or a virus can infect a previously virus-free program and turn it into a Trojan Horse. The possibilities are limited by the devious minds of the people who create these programs.

NOTE *The most well-known worm was launched across the Internet computer network by a Cornell graduate student, effectively bringing to a grinding halt the system that links thousands of computers in government and universities. The student was subsequently arrested and put on trial for violating computer trespass laws. In his defense, the student—ironically, the son of a government security expert—claimed he'd launched the worm to show just how at-risk the Internet system was. He was found guilty and sentenced to a term of probation and public service.*

Infectious programs in any of these forms generally are created by pranksters who want to show off their programming skills—and wreak havoc while they're at it.

VIRUS DETECTION

Just as you have to come in contact with someone who has a virus in order to be infected, a computer must come in contact with a virus-infected computer or program in order for it to be infected. Usually, computer viruses are spread in a few common ways:

▶ *By copying a contaminated program onto your PC from a floppy disk*

▶ *By directly connecting to an infected computer via either a direct cable link or a modem connection, copying the infected program, and running it on your computer*

▶ *By downloading an infected program from a bulletin board system*

▶ *By sharing files across a local area network*

▶ *By an overt and malicious act of an individual*

Your computer may be infected by a virus for some time before you experience any symptoms. But once the virus becomes active, there are several sure signs of infection.

THE TYPES OF VIRUSES

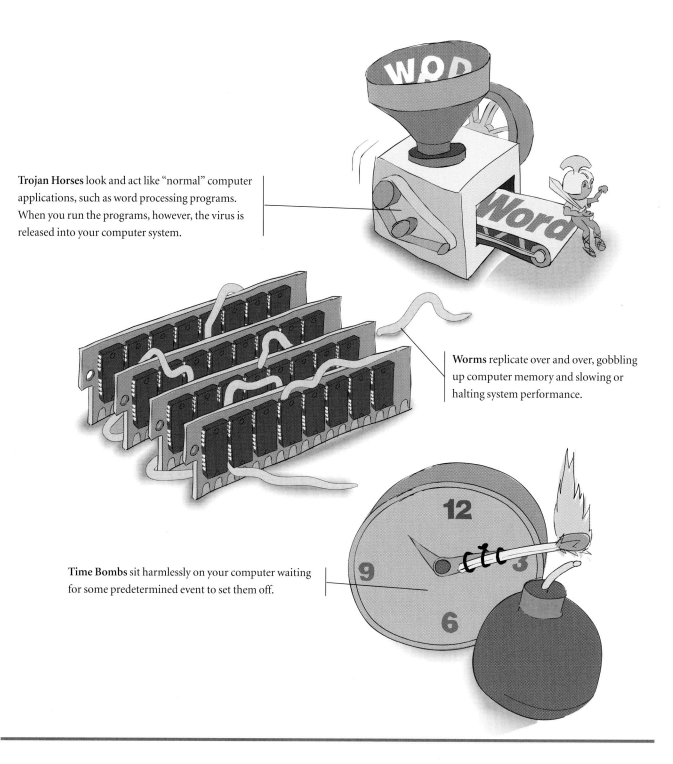

Trojan Horses look and act like "normal" computer applications, such as word processing programs. When you run the programs, however, the virus is released into your computer system.

Worms replicate over and over, gobbling up computer memory and slowing or halting system performance.

Time Bombs sit harmlessly on your computer waiting for some predetermined event to set them off.

Perhaps the most overt sign of a virus is an unexpected or unusual message popping up on your computer screen when you use a program or are at the DOS prompt. Some messages are playful, if still annoying. The Joker virus, for example, flashes a message announcing its need to be fed hamburgers through the floppy-disk drive. Other viruses suddenly play strains of "Yankee Doodle Dandy" through the computer speaker or cause letters to randomly drop to the bottom of the screen. You might get a message that looks like a legitimate error message, but appears in a program or operation that has always run flawlessly in the past. Check your application or DOS manual. If the message is not documented there, it could be a sign of a virus. And beware: If the message even hints that it will erase or format your hard disk, and especially if the hard-disk access light comes on, turn off the computer immediately and don't turn it on again until you can reboot from a clean DOS disk. In some cases, this might be enough to save your data.

Another sign of infection is an application that always ran without trouble acting unusual or crashing unexpectedly. The keyboard may become inactive or the hard-disk access light may come on frequently, even if you aren't retrieving or storing a file. Sometimes, the computer may even reboot unexpectedly.

If programs begin to take significantly longer to load than they usually do, a virus may be up to some dirty trick. Triggered by launching a program, a virus can take over the start-up procedure of the host application, replicating itself and beginning its damaging mission. Maybe your application launches just fine, but as you work your PC runs more and more slowly. A worm could be replicating and eating up available random-access memory (RAM) that the application would otherwise use to run more efficiently.

Viruses can exhibit themselves by deleting files or by creating new files on your hard disk. If you notice that files you have saved are no longer on your hard disk, or new files you never created make a guest appearance, you may have an infection.

When a virus attaches itself to a program file, the size of the file gets larger. You might notice that you have less hard-drive storage than you expect or that a program

DETECTING VIRUSES

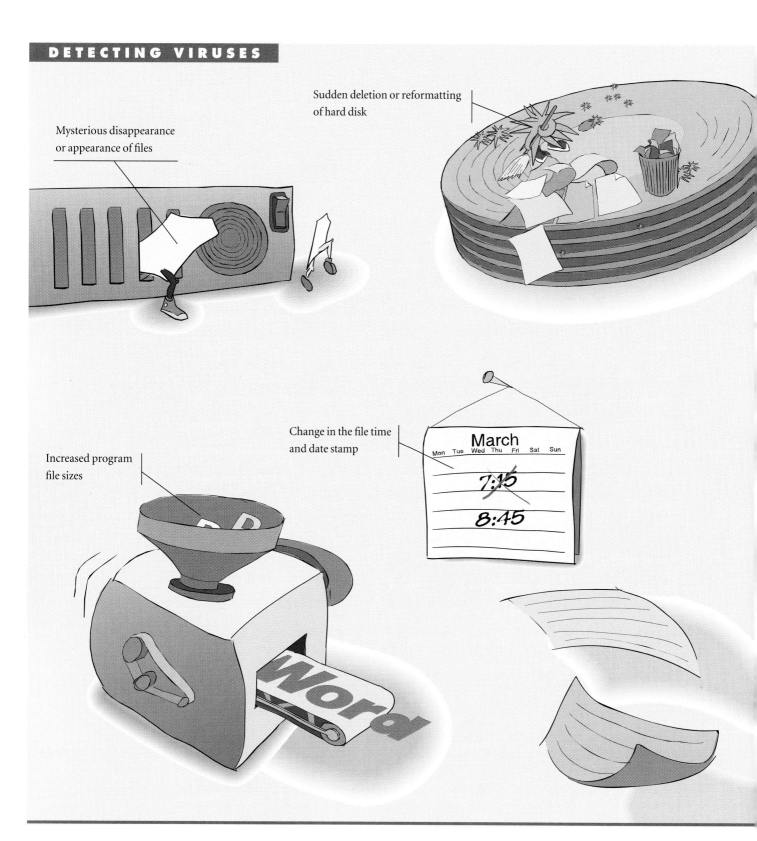

Mysterious disappearance or appearance of files

Sudden deletion or reformatting of hard disk

Increased program file sizes

Change in the file time and date stamp

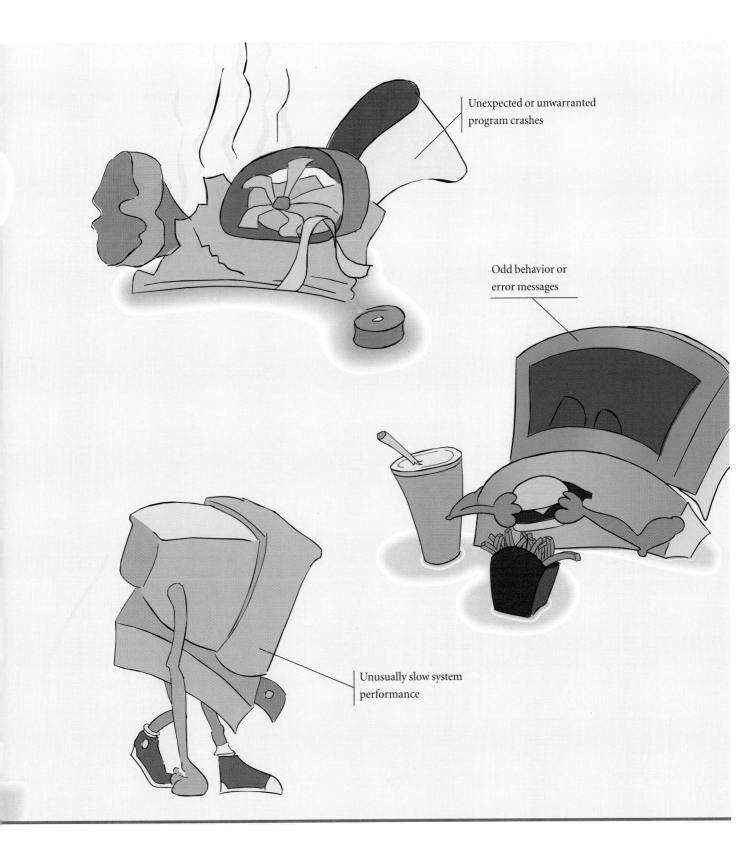

Unexpected or unwarranted program crashes

Odd behavior or error messages

Unusually slow system performance

that once took 100 kilobytes (K), for example, now requires 105K of storage. This is a sign that a virus has infected the program and may be replicating itself.

All files—program or data—have a time and date stamp that indicates when they were created or last changed. You can see the time and date stamp when you type DIR at a DOS prompt and get a list of all files on the floppy or hard-disk drive. When you run an application, the date stamp does not change unless the program has in some way been altered (normal changes to program configuration, such as changing display colors, do not change the application's date stamp). If the date stamp of an application changes, this may indicate that a virus has infected the program and modified it. Periodically using the DIR command to check the time and date stamp on program files can alert you to a virus.

You might experience one of these symptoms without actually having a virus. In fact, often it is something other than a virus that is causing problems on your computer. But if you experience one of these symptoms, it's wise to immediately assume the worst—you have a virus. Attempt to identify it and cure the problem.

Imagine that your hard-disk light begins flashing and strange messages dance across the screen. Sure signs of a virus, but what do you do now? First and foremost, don't panic. Take a deep breath and follow these simple steps:

▶ *Turn off your computer. Save whatever you have been working on (your work may be lost to the virus, but it's always a good bet to try to save it), and then shut off your computer. If you have floppy disks in the drives, remove them and note on their labels (using a soft tip pen) that they may be infected with a virus. If you have any sort of removable hard disk or tape cartridge, do the same with these.*

▶ *Reboot from a clean DOS disk. Using the original DOS disk that came with your PC, start up your computer. Be sure the DOS disk is write protected. On 5 ¼-inch floppy disks the notch in the upper-right corner should be covered with a write-protect tab or even a piece of tape. Some original boot disks have no notch at all.*

For 3 ½-inch disks, slide the plastic tab on the back left corner of the disk upward to reveal a square hole. Booting from a clean DOS disk ensures that the virus isn't hiding in the PC's system memory, still able to infect other files.

▶ *Use an antivirus program to find the virus. There are both commercial antivirus programs, such as Symantec's Norton AntiVirus or the antivirus utilities that come with MS-DOS 6.0 and PC-DOS 6.1, and shareware antivirus programs, such as McAfee's Viruscan, for ferreting out viruses. Any of these programs will work well. Run them from a write-protected floppy disk to scan your hard- and floppy-disk drives to determine the source of infection.*

▶ *Repair or delete infected files. Should these antivirus programs identify a virus, immediately try to repair or delete the affected files. Most antivirus packages include a program that will attempt to repair the file by deleting just the virus code from infected programs. If a virus cannot be eliminated from the program, delete the entire file (you should be able to restore program files from your original installation disks) using either the antivirus program or the DOS DEL command.*

▶ *Rescan the drive that had the virus program. Once you have repaired and/or deleted infected files, use the antivirus program to scan your hard and floppy disks again to make sure that you have completely eradicated the source of the problem.*

▶ *Scan all floppy disks and backup files for signs of the virus. Don't trust that just because you've found and eliminated the virus on your hard disk, you're through with it. Use the antivirus program to scan every floppy disk you have, especially backup disks that were made directly from your hard disk. This will help to ensure that you aren't reinfected, and it may identify the source of the original virus. Furthermore, if you're certain your backup files aren't infected with the virus, you can use them to restore files you may have lost on your hard disk. If you do this,*

TROUBLESHOOTING VIRUSES

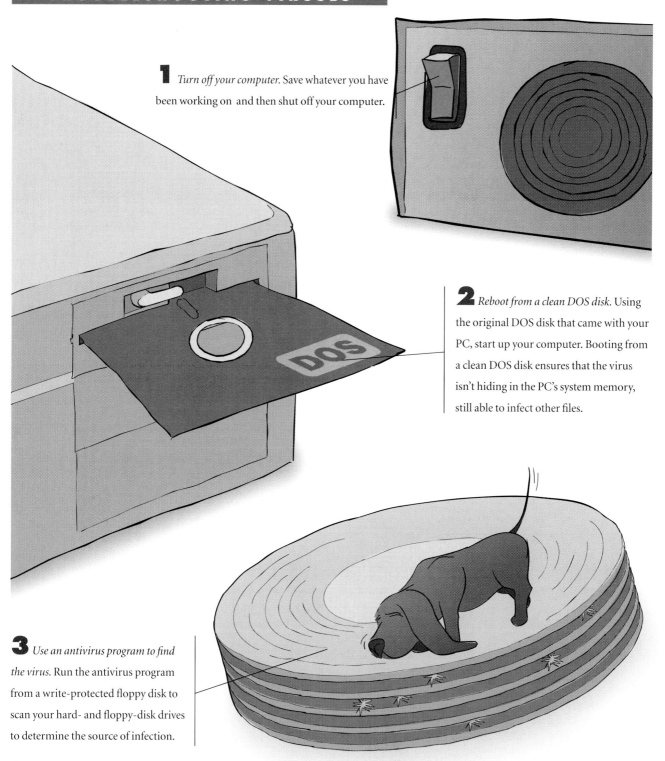

1 *Turn off your computer.* Save whatever you have been working on and then shut off your computer.

2 *Reboot from a clean DOS disk.* Using the original DOS disk that came with your PC, start up your computer. Booting from a clean DOS disk ensures that the virus isn't hiding in the PC's system memory, still able to infect other files.

3 *Use an antivirus program to find the virus.* Run the antivirus program from a write-protected floppy disk to scan your hard- and floppy-disk drives to determine the source of infection.

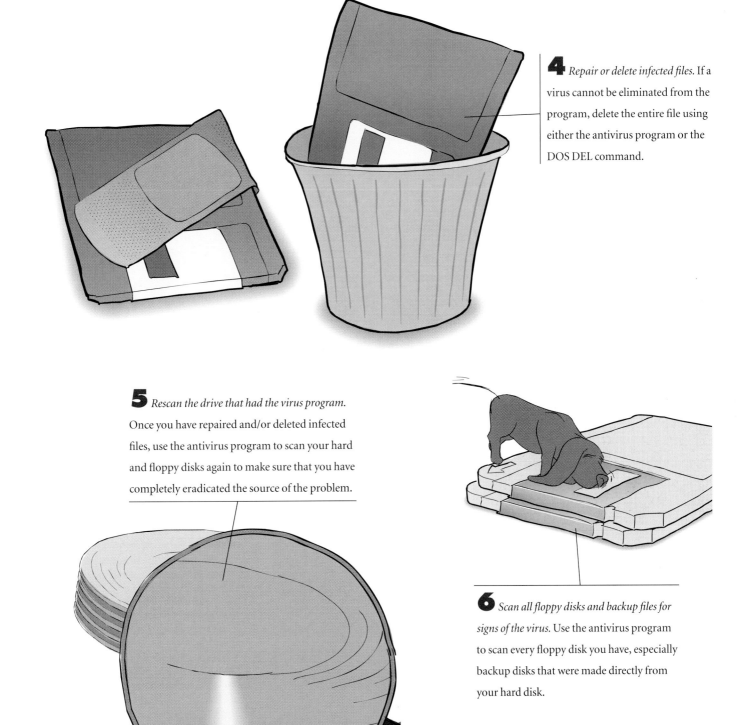

4 *Repair or delete infected files.* If a virus cannot be eliminated from the program, delete the entire file using either the antivirus program or the DOS DEL command.

5 *Rescan the drive that had the virus program.* Once you have repaired and/or deleted infected files, use the antivirus program to scan your hard and floppy disks again to make sure that you have completely eradicated the source of the problem.

6 *Scan all floppy disks and backup files for signs of the virus.* Use the antivirus program to scan every floppy disk you have, especially backup disks that were made directly from your hard disk.

play it safe and scan your hard disk once again after you've restored your files and then again every couple of weeks until you are sure you are virus free.

If all your best efforts can't identify and cure the virus, get expert help. Call the National Computer Security Association (717-258-1816). It's there to help computer users deal with viruses.

Once you have found and eliminated the virus, you may want to take an extra precaution to be sure the virus is absolutely wiped out. The one sure way to do this is to reformat your hard disk, and then reinstall your applications programs from their original installation disks. If you do decide to take this extra measure, be sure to back up all your data files to new floppy disks. Viruses don't infect data files, so these are safe to copy onto a newly formatted hard disk without fear of reintroducing the nasty virus. Once you've copied your data onto floppy disks, refer to your DOS manual for instructions on reformatting your hard disk, and then follow those instructions carefully.

N O T E *The* Computer Virus Survival Guide, *available from the National Computer Security Association, is a quick reference that includes tips for virus prevention and recovery. It's available for $5 by writing to NCSA, 10 South Courthouse Ave., Carlisle, PA 17013. An updated version of this pamphlet, retitled* Norman's Computer Virus Survival Guide, *costs about $20. For more information, contact Norman Data Defense Systems, 2775-B Harland Road, Falls Church, VA 22043, (703) 573-8802.*

Virus Prevention

It isn't hard to protect your computer system against viruses. Just follow these basic rules:

Tip 1: **USE ONLY SOFTWARE THAT COMES IN ITS ORIGINAL SHRINK-WRAPPED PACKAGE.** Software developers ensure that the programs they provide to customers are free from viruses. If you use the original program disks to install software onto your PC, you can be sure you won't get a virus. It might be tempting to use copies of software someone else has purchased rather than buying a package yourself—these copies are called *pirated software.* Copying original program disks to newly formatted floppy disks may not increase your computer's chances of getting a virus, but it violates the terms of the original licensing agreement and is illegal. Moreover, unless you've made the copy yourself (an illegal act), you can't be sure where else those disks have been.

Tip 2: **USE AN ANTIVIRUS PROGRAM TO SCAN FLOPPY DISKS** *before* you copy them to your computer. Unless you are absolutely certain of the source of a floppy disk, and you know it to be free of viruses, it's wise to scan the disk before installing or copying that disk to your hard disk. Scan any programs you download from bulletin boards and any disks that friends might pass along to you. More viruses are spread by coworkers and friends sharing floppy disks than by files downloaded from bulletin boards.

Tip 3: **AVOID DOWNLOADING FILES FROM UNKNOWN BULLETIN BOARD SYSTEMS.** Downloading software (copying a program from an on-line service or bulletin board system) is a great way to build your software library. But stick to on-line services and bulletin boards that are well known or recommended by others who have successfully used them. All major on-line services and any legitimate bulletin board operator scan software programs to be sure they are safe before making them available for downloading. If you'd like to try a new bulletin board, leave a message for the board operator inquiring about the bulletin board's virus-protection procedures *before* you download from that service. If you do download software from a new service, download the program and scan it immediately with an antivirus program. If the scan turns up a virus, delete the program immediately. (Remember, you can only get a virus from a bulletin board by downloading and *running* a program. It's absolutely safe to dial into a bulletin board and read and leave messages—these activities can't cause you to get a virus.)

Tip 4: **MAKE REGULAR BACKUPS OF YOUR HARD DISK.** One of the best ways to overcome a disastrous virus infection is to be prepared for it. By regularly making complete backups of your hard disk, you will be able to quickly recover from a virus attack. Of course, if you do suffer from a virus, be certain to scan your backups to be sure they are virus free. And even without the threat of viruses, hard-disk backups are a good idea. To be sure, more data is lost to mechanical failures of the hard disk than to viruses.

Tip 5: **WRITE-PROTECT YOUR COMMAND.COM FILE.** The COMMAND.COM file in your hard disk's root directory is a primary target for viruses. You can protect this file by using the DOS ATTRIB command to change the file's status to read only. To do this, type **ATTRIB +R C:\COMMAND.COM** at the DOS prompt. (If you later need to change the status of COMMAND.COM back to read and write status, simply type **ATTRIB -R C:\COMMAND.COM** at the DOS prompt.)

If you want extra insurance that you'll not get infected, you will want to invest in an antivirus package that includes a memory-resident module that conscientiously watches new program files to ensure they are virus-free and to intercept and eradicate viruses if they aren't. Of course, memory-resident software requires extra system resources, including random-access memory in which to run. This might cause other applications to run more slowly and in some cases not leave enough memory for larger applications to run at all. Another downside to these virus watchdog programs is that they must be updated regularly to keep up to date with new viruses as they are discovered. To help you keep pace, some antivirus software publishers, such as Symantec and Central Point, provide services that send regular updates to you via disk or through their own bulletin boards.

MYTHS AND TRUTHS ABOUT VIRUSES

As the most high-profile danger of personal computing, viruses are prone to a lot of misunderstanding. Not that we should feel sorry for the poor, misunderstood virus, mind you. But separating virus fact from fiction will make you less likely to come in contact with these nasty programs.

Myth 1: **VIRUSES ARE EVERYWHERE, EVERYWHERE!** It's true that many new viruses and variations on old ones are discovered nearly every day. But the relatively low number of virus attacks suggests this is not a problem of epidemic proportions. A couple of years ago, IBM conducted a survey of its big customers and discovered that only about one computer in 1,000 was hit with a virus in a three-month period. And there's little evidence to conclude that number has grown significantly.

Myth 2: **VIRUSES SPREAD OVER BULLETIN BOARD SYSTEMS.** Actually, just dialing into a bulletin board won't give you a virus. You must download infected software and run it on your computer before the virus will take hold and spread. Even then, legitimate bulletin boards and on-line services scan their downloadable files and software to ensure that they are free from viruses. In fact, you are more likely to get a virus from programs shared by floppy disk than from software you download from a bulletin board system.

Myth 3: **IF I GET A VIRUS, EVERYTHING IS LOST.** Cleaning up after a virus strikes is no fun, to be sure. But suffering a virus doesn't necessarily mean your computer and data are a total loss. First, a virus can't damage the electronic and mechanical workings of a computer. Once the virus is cleaned off the system, the computer is as good as new. Second, a virus can cause damage to data by erasing files, for example, but it can't infect the data itself. So long as you have a backup copy of your hard disk, it's likely you'll be able to recover any data a virus might attack.

Myth 4: **I'M NOT LIKELY TO GET A VIRUS, SO WHY WORRY ABOUT IT.** It's true that the chances of your computer being infected by a virus are relatively slim. Nevertheless, it's important not to write them off as a hoax that can't affect you. The best rule of thumb is to be aware of the risks, protect yourself, but, of course, don't become so preoccupied by the risk that you don't enjoy the adventures awaiting you on bulletin boards and on-line services.

PREVENTING VIRUSES

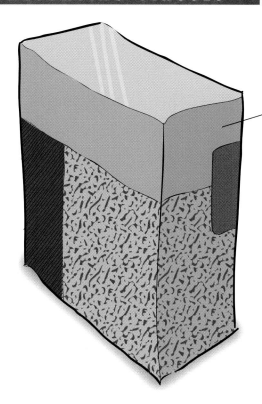

Use only software that comes in its original shrink-wrapped package.

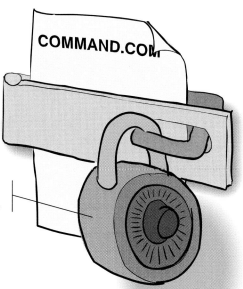

Write-protect your COMMAND.COM file.

Use an antivirus program to scan floppy disks before you run the programs they contain.

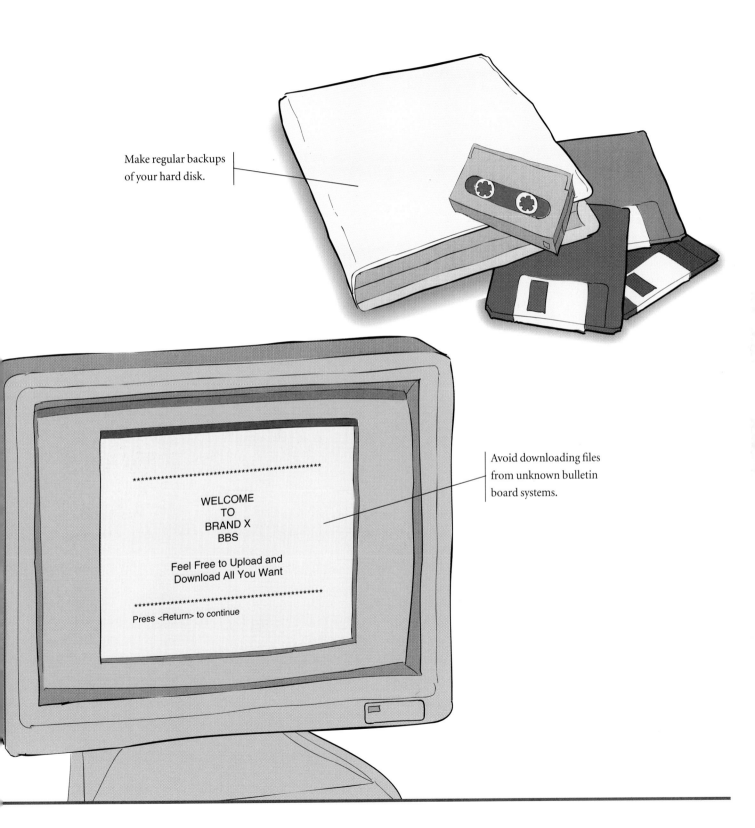

Make regular backups
of your hard disk.

Avoid downloading files
from unknown bulletin
board systems.

```
************************************************
              WELCOME
                TO
             BRAND X
               BBS

        Feel Free to Upload and
        Download All You Want

************************************************
Press <Return> to continue
```

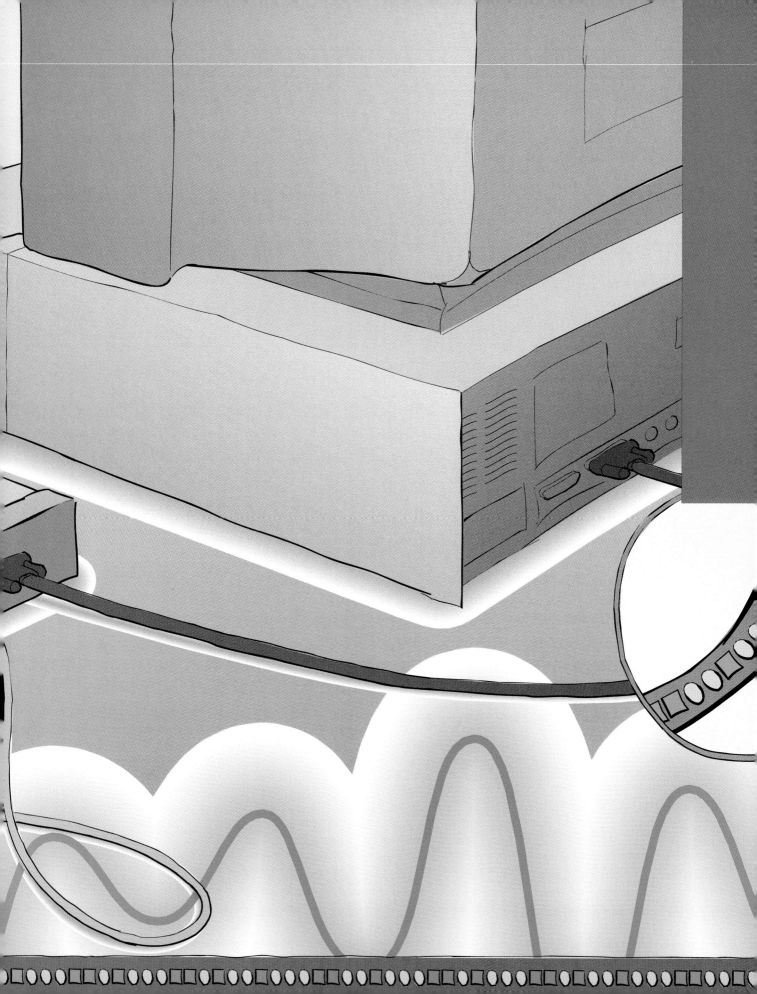

4

WHAT YOU NEED TO GET CONNECTED

How Modems Work

What to Look for in a Modem

Understanding Your Phone Line

Communications Software

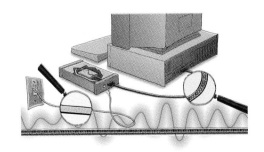

4

Getting connected is a lot easier than most people think. In fact, it requires only a PC, modem, phone line, and communications software. Each of these plays an important and necessary role in getting on line. The PC and communications software work together as the command station for the whole operation. The modem is the go-between for the PC and the telephone system, and the phone line is the pathway across which information travels. Without one, the others are absolutely useless in communicating information on line. So just how do they all work? And how do they work together?

HOW MODEMS WORK

Have you ever been in a foreign country where you didn't speak the language? Wonderful conversations happen all around you. A young woman enthusiastically recommends a great neighborhood bistro. A shopper describes the terrific bargains at an out-of-the-way boutique. Two friends laugh at a shared joke. A stockbroker whispers a tip on a sure investment. And you don't understand any of it. You need a translator.

That's how it is for computers and telephones. They speak different languages and can't understand one another without a translator. A modem is that translator. Computers understand only *digital information*—electronic signals that represent one of two positions: on or off. It's the combination of these on-off signals that represents information to a computer. Telephones, on the other hand, understand only *analog tones*—continuous sound waves that move over wires or through the air. The trouble comes because digital and analog machines—PCs and phones, in this case—can't understand one another directly because they speak different languages. Without a translator the computer can't understand information sent over telephone lines.

The word modem stands for MOdulator/DEModulator. When you send information from your PC, the modem converts (modulates) digital signals coming from your PC to analog signals that can be sent over telephone lines. When you receive information, the modem converts (demodulates) the analog tones from the phone line back into digital signals the computer can understand.

Though all this sounds complicated (and there is a bit of technical wizardry inside a modem), the modem itself is a pretty simple device. Its sole purpose is to act as the go-between between your computer and the phone, making sure the two can understand one another.

WHAT TO LOOK FOR IN A MODEM

Modems come in several flavors, but your choice will be determined by three things: compatibility, design, and speed.

Compatibility is the easiest to deal with of these three issues. You need to choose a modem that is compatible with your computer, and that's a cinch because nearly a hundred percent of all modems will work with both IBM-compatible and Macintosh computers. In most cases, you'll simply need to ask your computer salesperson for the appropriate style of connector cable depending on whether you're using a PC or a Mac.

You may also hear something about AT compatibility in modems. In the early days of personal computers, Hayes Microcomputer Products developed a set of commands that let software tell modems what to do. These commands are called the *AT command set*. Because Hayes sold so many modems that used the AT command set, and because communications software makers rapidly took advantage of the command set to make their programs more useful, many more modem makers began selling what they called *Hayes-compatible*, or *AT-compatible*, modems. Today, it is virtually impossible to buy a PC modem that is not Hayes-compatible. I mention it here only because you may come across the term, and this nugget of information will keep you out of the dark. (I'll talk more about the AT command set in Chapter 5.)

DIGITAL SIGNALS VERSUS ANALOG SIGNALS

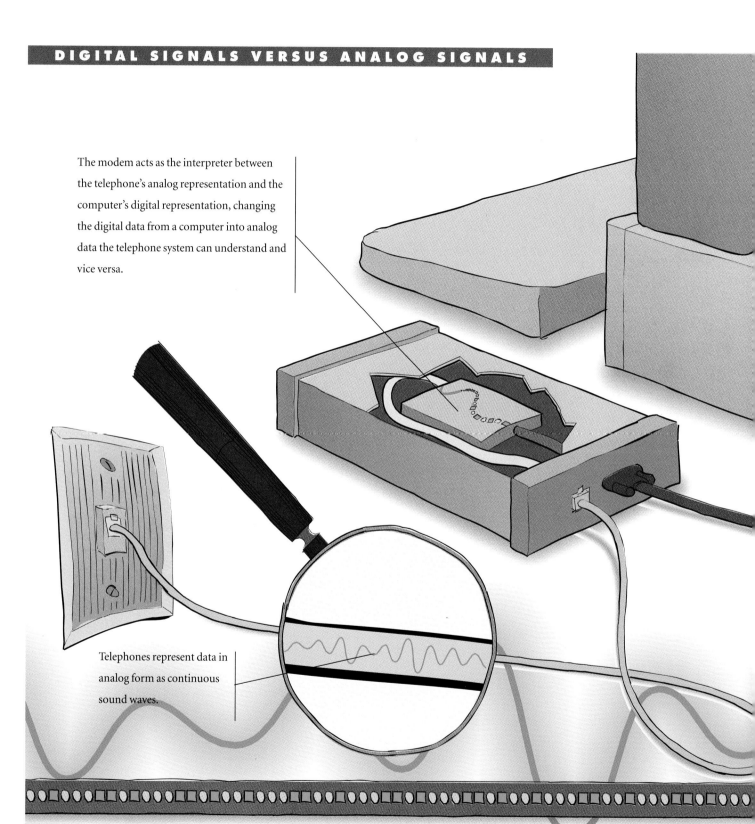

The modem acts as the interpreter between the telephone's analog representation and the computer's digital representation, changing the digital data from a computer into analog data the telephone system can understand and vice versa.

Telephones represent data in analog form as continuous sound waves.

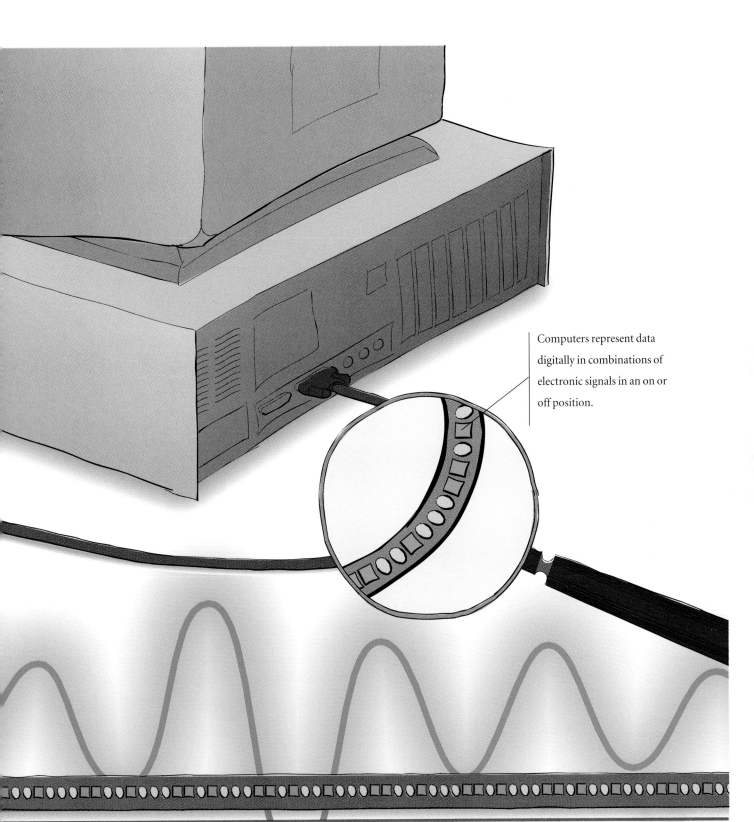

Computers represent data digitally in combinations of electronic signals in an on or off position.

INTERNAL VERSUS EXTERNAL MODEMS

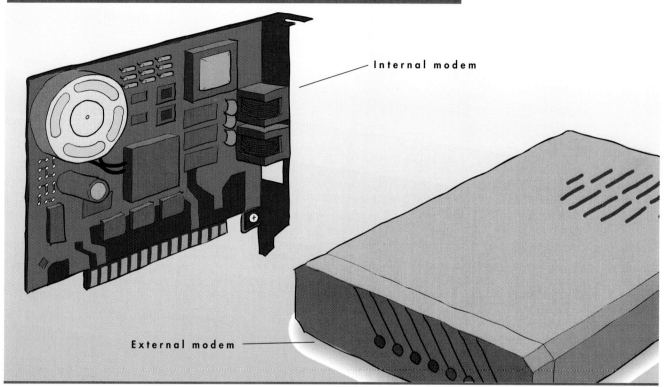

Internal modem

External modem

With compatibility out of the way, you can focus on the more important distinctions. Modems are designed in one of two ways: They are either *internal* (installed inside your computer) or *external* (attached to the outside of your PC). Internal modems take the form of a circuit board that fits inside your computer. An internal modem requires an *expansion slot*, which is simply a connection between any circuit board and the PC's main processing system. Expansion slots are used for a variety of purposes—storage devices, a mouse, a scanner, sound systems, and so on. Each of these things can require an expansion slot. If all the slots have been used for another purpose, you'll need to use an external modem rather than an internal one. External modems are usually a flat box about the size of a book that houses the circuit board and connects to your PC with a cable. Both types of modems do the same job. The type you choose depends largely on whether you have available space inside your PC.

COMPARING MODEM SPEEDS

A 9,600 bps modem can send up to eight times more data per second than a 1,200 bps modem and four times more than a 2,400 bps modem. When you are sending and receiving lots of information, that speed can make a dramatic difference in the amount of time you spend online.

Incidentally, more and more PCs come with an internal modem preinstalled. If your computer included a modem when you bought it, the dirty work of installing the modem has been done for you, and you can skip right past this section of the chapter.

Once you've determined whether your modem will be internal or external, you'll need to know a bit about its speed. A modem's speed determines how quickly it can send and receive data. Essentially, the faster the modem, the faster it can translate the PC's digital signals into analog signals and stuff them down the phone line. Modem speeds are rated by the bits (or individual pieces of data) that the modem can send to the phone line in one second. This rating is called *bits per second*, or *bps*. Modem speed is also measured in *kilobits per second*, or *kbps*.

NOTE *The term bits per second is sometimes confused with the term* baud. *Baud rate has to do with the telephone line itself and refers to the number of signal changes that can take place in a second.*

While modems come in a variety of speeds, the most common speeds for personal computers are 2,400 bps, 9,600 bps, and 14.4 kbps (usually called "fourteen dot four"). Obviously, the faster the modem, the more quickly information is sent from and received by your PC, and the less time you spend waiting for information to arrive. Fast modems, such as 9,600 bps modems, can talk to slower modems by slowing the speed at which they send and receive information. But under normal circumstances no modem can talk faster than its rated speed. For example, a 2,400 bps modem can talk to a 9,600 bps modem because the 9,600 bps modem will slow down for it. But a 2,400 bps modem can't send data faster than 2,400 bits of information in one second. For a 9,600 bps modem to work at its fastest, it must be talking to another 9,600 bps modem or to one rated even faster. However, what should be a simple truth with computers—a modem can't send information faster than its rated speed—is not always strictly true. A modem *can* send more data per second than its rating by compressing the information. Using special techniques, the modem can squeeze information that might take 100 bits in a normal form to just 70 bits in compressed form, for example. As a result, a modem rated at 14.4 kbps and designed to send 14.4 kilobits of data per second might actually be able to send 30 kilobits worth of data per second by compressing the information into fewer bits.

The ability to send information this quickly depends a lot on the quality of the telephone line. Sometimes when you make a telephone call, the connection is crystal clear. Other times, you hear a lot of static or clicking on the line. You can overlook this so-called line noise when you're talking to someone on the phone, but a modem can't. It tries to interpret everything it "hears" coming across the line. When data is being sent slowly, say at 2,400 bps, the modem has an easier time differentiating data from noise. At faster speeds, say at 9,600 bps, the task of separating noise from data becomes much harder. As a result, the modem may make a mistake and interpret line noise as data. Fortunately, most modems today are self-correcting, using something called an error correction protocol. Error correction protocols can be quite complex. Suffice it to say that

MODEMS CAN'T TALK FASTER THAN THEIR RATED SPEED

In order to achieve optimum speeds, a 9,600 bps modem, for example, must connect to another 9,600 bps modem (top). But a fast modem can slow down in order to communicate with a slower modem (bottom).

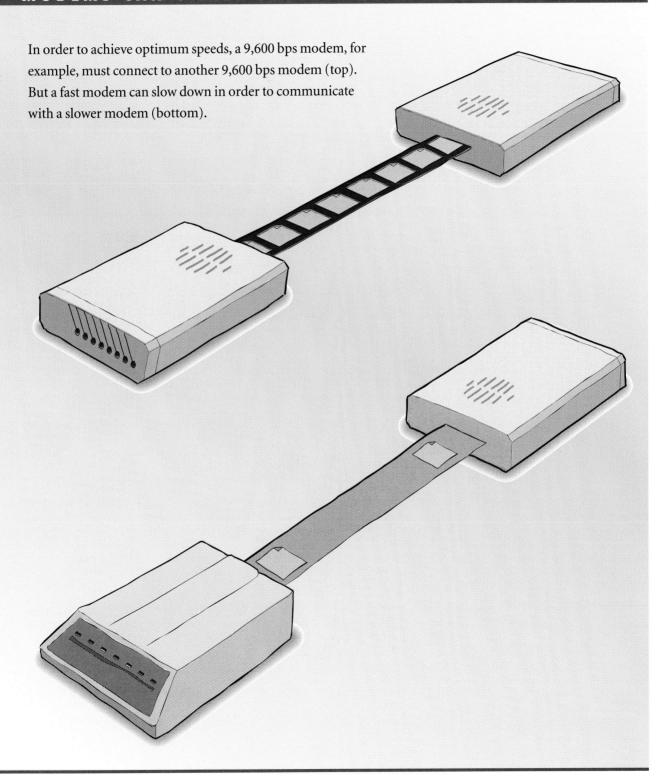

the modems on either end of the connection compare notes on what one has sent with what the other has received. If their notes don't match, the sending modem will resend that data in question.

ERROR CORRECTION PROTOCOLS

There is no need for you to get bogged down in error correction protocols, but it is important for you to know what kind of error correction your modem uses. Some of the more popular methods are MNP5, v.42, and v.42bis. For error correction protocols to work, the modems on both ends of the connection need to use the same protocol. Many bulletin boards and on-line services have access numbers for modems using different error correction protocols. By knowing what type of error correction your modem uses, you can choose the best access number when you dial into these services.

Fax Modems   As you shop for a modem, you may hear the term *fax modem* or *data/fax modem*. The words mean the same thing: a modem that can handle both data *and* fax transmissions. While a fax modem looks no different from a standard data-only modem, it has the ability to communicate with office fax machines and other fax modems. Even if you don't need fax capabilities right now, you might want to consider buying a fax modem rather than a data-only modem—*just in case*. Typically, a fax modem costs only a little more than a standard data modem, and often the fax software you need to send and/or receive faxes with your computer is included in the price.

There are several types of fax modems, but the differences are pretty basic. First, some fax modems can only send faxes—they can't receive them. If you want to receive incoming faxes with your computer, you should be sure the fax modem has *send* and *receive* capabilities, and these days most fax modems do. Secondly, be sure your fax modem is at least Group 3 compatible, or better yet, Group 4 compatible. Group 3 and Group 4 are fax standards and determine the speed at which a fax is sent, among other things. Group 3 and Group 4 fax modems are able to talk to one another. It's just that a Group 4 fax modem will communicate more quickly with another Group 4 fax modem or fax machine than it will with a Group 3-compatible device. Finally, you may want to look for a *CAS-compatible* modem. CAS, or Communications Application Specification, was developed by Intel and defines how most software applications communicate with fax software. Your fax modem doesn't have to be CAS-compatible, but you may find it a big convenience because CAS will allow you to fax a document without leaving the application in which you created it.

To use a fax modem, however, you must have special fax communications software. This software allows you to send almost any document created by a word processor, graphics program, spreadsheet, or other application to a fax machine anywhere in the world. Generally, the fax software intercepts selected documents heading to the printer and saves them in a file as a graphic image of the document as it would have looked on the printed page. Once the file is captured, you direct the fax software to prepare a cover page, append the document image file, dial a fax number, and send the document. At the receiving end, the cover page and document look just like an incoming call from another fax machine. In fact, the document typically looks *better* than if you had printed it and fed it into a fax machine because often graphic clarity is lost in the translations from the electronic file to the fax printout.

Just as with ordinary data modems, fax modems also come in external and internal models. Fax modems are installed in the same way as data-only modems.

UNDERSTANDING YOUR PHONE LINE

What would you possibly need to know about phone lines? After all, there's just an outlet in the wall into which you plug your phone, right? It's almost that simple. That outlet in your wall leads to an intricate web of phone systems connecting with one another, much like an on-ramp leads to a highway that connects to many other roads and highways. That may seem obvious enough, but like highways, not all phone systems are the same. The first thing (and likely the last) you need to know about phone lines is what kind of phone system you have.

Essentially, there are two kinds of phone systems: touch tone and pulse. The majority of phone systems in the United States are touch tone, which means that each number is represented by a different pitch or tone. Pulse phone systems send a series of electronic pulses to represent a number—five pulses for the number five, for example—rather than sending a tone for each number.

Your modem will work with either touch-tone or pulse systems, but you'll need to know which type you have. To make this determination, pick up your phone and press the number 5. If you hear a musical note, you have a touch-tone phone line. If you hear five clicks, you have a pulse system.

The second thing you'll need to know about your phone line is whether you have call waiting. Call waiting is a convenience in voice calls that alerts you to incoming calls. But it's a major inconvenience when it interrupts—and cuts off—your modem connection. You can avoid these interruptions by suspending call waiting during your modem communications sessions. Just add the digits 1170 to the beginning of the number you want the modem to dial. Then incoming calls get a standard busy signal and you have a connection free of unwanted interruptions. Once you hang up your modem, the call waiting feature is resumed for subsequent calls.

COMMUNICATIONS SOFTWARE

If modems are the translators between PCs and phone lines, and phone lines are the highways across which information is sent, then communications software is the glue that holds it all together. Communications software tells the modem what telephone number to dial, what sort of computer to expect at the other end, and how to talk to it. Communications software is also your window into the on-line connection.

Communications programs handle basic functions such as dialing a phone number, sending text, and receiving text and other information. But communications software can have other, more advanced features, too. Typically, communications software includes a telephone directory where you enter the information and phone number of the on-line services and bulletin boards you use. The software may also have a mini word processor that you can use to compose messages. When you are connected to a service or bulletin board, the communications software acts as the go-between, telling you what information the on-line connection is requesting and relaying your commands back to the service. Some communications packages even have a *scripting language* that lets you write out and store instructions so that your software can automatically call on-line services without your intervention.

N O T E *If your computer came equipped with a modem already installed in it, it probably also came with communications software. If your PC runs the Windows graphical interface, you have a simple communications program in the Windows Terminal application.*

Many on-line services, such as the Prodigy Information Service and America On-line, have their own communications software that you'll need in order to use these services. Other on-line services, such as GEnie and CompuServe, can be used with any communications packages. Still, there are several programs, such as WinCIM and TAP-CIS on the PC, and Navigator for the Mac, that are designed to work exclusively with CompuServe. These programs make getting around the large and complex information service much easier and much more cost-effective. I'll talk about some of these programs in Chapter 8, where I'll discuss on-line services in detail.

Communications capabilities are also built into many other kinds of software. For example, the personal finance programs you read about in Chapter 1 include communications software for dialing into bill-paying systems, such as Checkfree, or into on-line services to gather stock quotes. Address-book programs might include a communications component that instructs the PC to dial a phone number for you.

THE KEY FEATURES OF YOUR CONNECTION

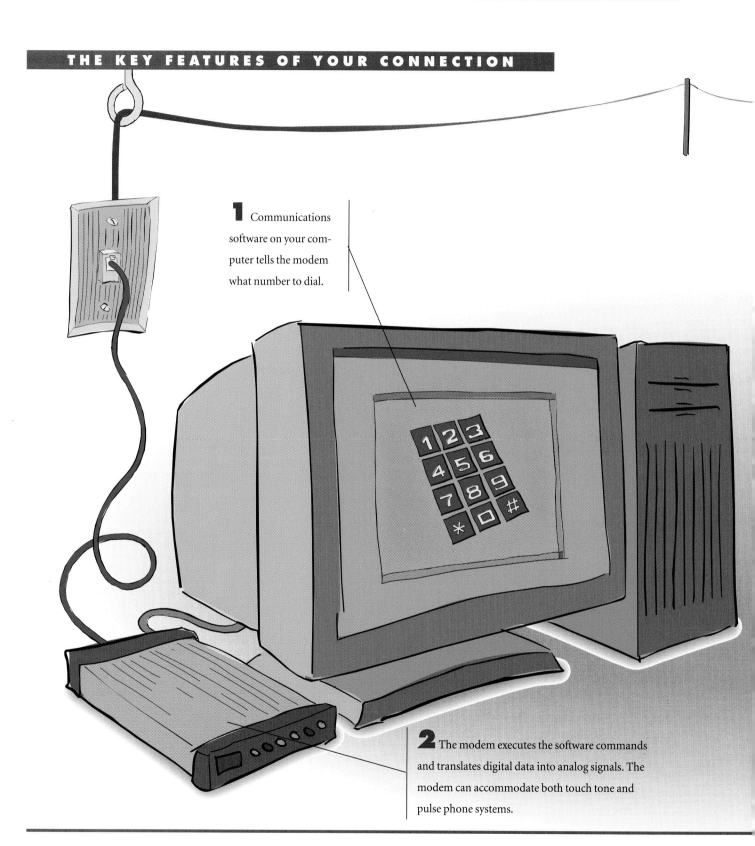

1 Communications software on your computer tells the modem what number to dial.

2 The modem executes the software commands and translates digital data into analog signals. The modem can accommodate both touch tone and pulse phone systems.

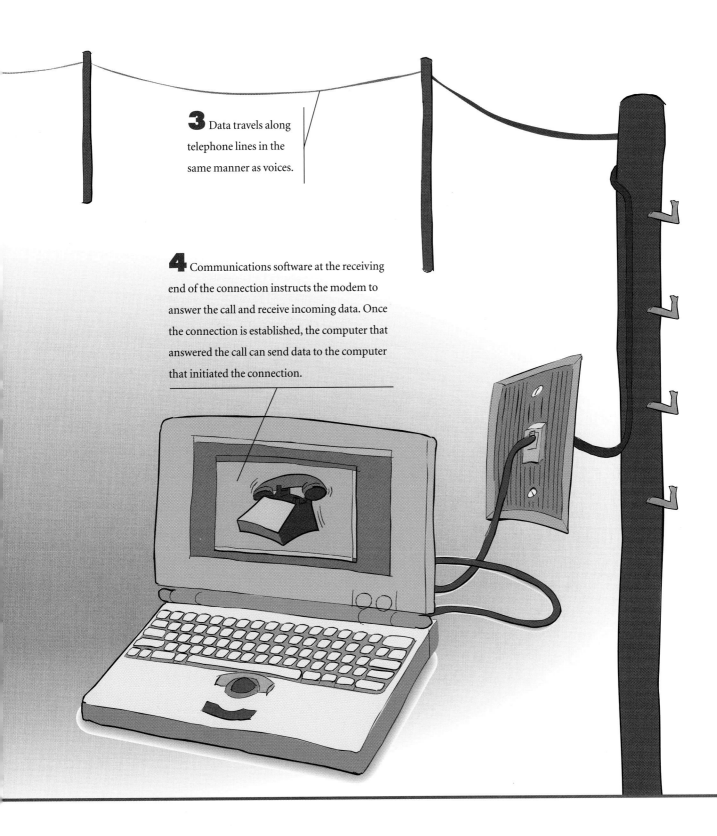

3 Data travels along telephone lines in the same manner as voices.

4 Communications software at the receiving end of the connection instructs the modem to answer the call and receive incoming data. Once the connection is established, the computer that answered the call can send data to the computer that initiated the connection.

5

GETTING READY TO CONNECT

Everything You Need to Know about DIP Switches

▪

Installing an External Modem

▪

Installing an Internal Modem

▪

Installing Communications Software

▪

Configuring Your Software

5

Have you ever purchased a new toy that comes in a box with "some assembly required" written across the top? You just want to tear into the box, toss the directions aside, and put the thing together. The impulse is the right one—you want to assemble the toy so you can start playing with it now. But the few minutes it takes to read the instructions, make sure all the parts are there, and put things in their proper places might save you hours of headache suffered while trying to figure out where those two leftover screws are supposed to go and why the thing doesn't really work as it is supposed to.

The same holds true for modems. Installing a modem is fairly easy, and you could probably figure it out without elaborate instructions. But take a few moments to read through this chapter to be sure your modem and communications software are installed to be trouble free.

EVERYTHING YOU NEED TO KNOW ABOUT DIP SWITCHES

Many modems include tiny on-off switches called DIP (dual in-line package) switches that let you change particular hardware functions from one state to another, for example, resetting the default modem settings, or telling the modem to automatically answer any incoming calls. The number and location of DIP switches varies from modem to modem and some modems may not have them at all. On an external modem, for example, the switches may be on the back of the unit, hidden behind a front face plate, or on the underside of the modem. On an internal modem, the switches may be on the modem board itself, where they can be reached after the modem is installed only by removing the computer's cover. Some manufacturers of internal modems have begun to place the DIP switches on the end-bracket that holds the modem in place and that is exposed to the outside of the computer. This is a much more convenient approach, as you can change the DIP switch settings without opening the computer.

WHAT YOU'LL NEED TO INSTALL YOUR MODEM

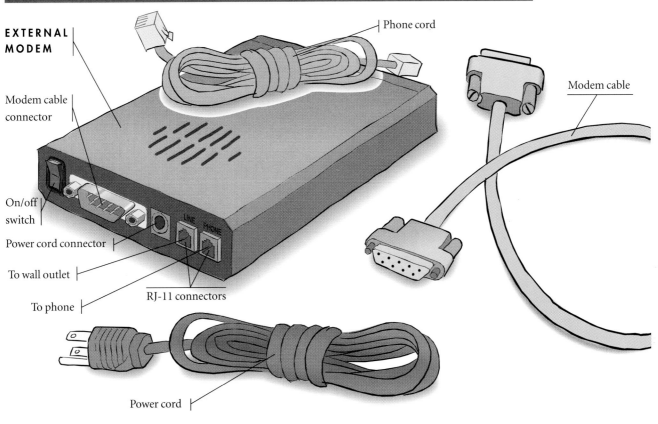

EXTERNAL
MODEM

Phone cord

Modem cable connector

Modem cable

On/off switch

Power cord connector

To wall outlet

To phone

LINE   PHONE

RJ-11 connectors

Power cord

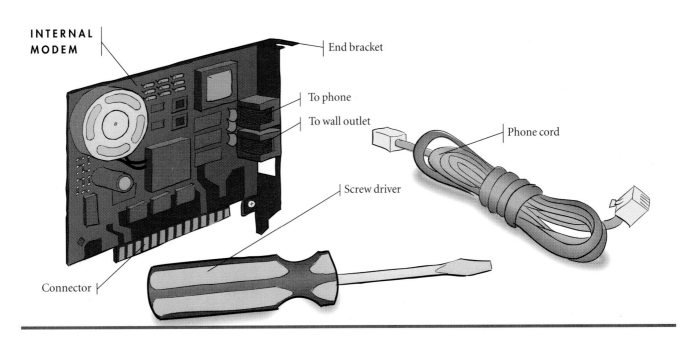

INTERNAL
MODEM

End bracket

To phone

To wall outlet

Phone cord

Screw driver

Connector

Your modem manual will outline the exact function of the DIP switches on your modem, and you should consult the manual before proceeding with installation. In nearly all cases, the factory settings of the DIP switches needn't be changed. Nevertheless, it's always better to set DIP switches *before* you install a board into your computer than to realize you need to change the setting after you have replaced the computer cover and screwed it back in place.

INSTALLING AN EXTERNAL MODEM

External and internal modems work identically, but the two are installed quite differently. As the names imply and as you've seen in Chapter 4, an external modem attaches to the outside of your computer and an internal modem is installed inside your computer. If you've not yet purchased a modem, you may want to consider the differences between external and internal modems and how they are installed before you make a choice. External modems typically cost a bit more than internal modems, usually about $50 to $100 more. The extra cost covers things an internal modem doesn't have or need, such as the modem case, a power supply, and the modem status lights. (Status lights are useful in telling you exactly what's going on when the modem is working.)

Because you don't have to open your computer's case to install an external modem, it is easier to install than an internal modem. Here's what you'll need to properly install an external modem: the modem, a phone cord, a serial cable, the modem's power cord, and an available port on your PC. Before you put these pieces together, however, check to be sure you have an available serial port to accommodate the modem cable connector. A serial port is an external connector through which the computer sends and receives information to and from external hardware devices, such as a modem or a mouse. Serial means the connector sends information one piece at a time, or as a series of bits. Hence the name *serial port*. Computers also have parallel ports, which connect to external devices, usually printers. Parallel ports send information several pieces at a time. You can tell the difference between serial and parallel ports easily—a serial port consists of two

A ROW OF DIP SWITCHES

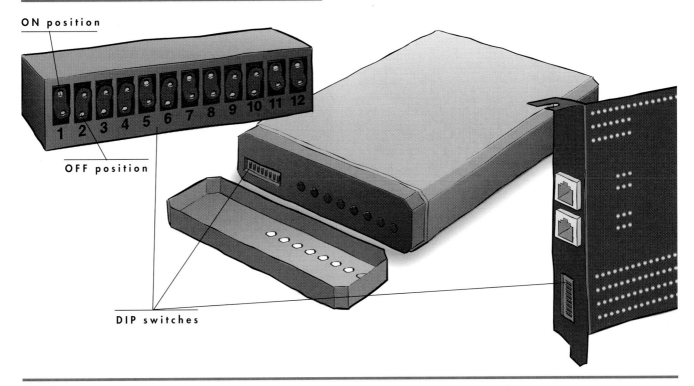

ON position

OFF position

DIP switches

rows of pins, and a parallel port has two rows of holes.

Serial ports can have either 9 or 25 pins. Either will work with an external modem. Just be sure your serial cable connector has the same number of holes as the port has pins. If it doesn't, you can get an adapter at any computer store.

The serial port or ports on your computer may be labeled COM1, COM2, and so on. It's best to use the first available serial port, COM1. That is the port the communications software will expect to use by default, unless you tell it otherwise (you'll learn more about that later). If your mouse, for example, is attached to the serial port labeled COM1, don't worry. You can use COM2 for your modem; just remember that you will have to let your communications software know where to look for the modem.

MAC Apple has made it easy for you to identify the Macintosh's serial port for modem communications by placing a phone symbol next to the proper port. Depending on the modem you choose, you'll install it easily by simply plugging the modem cable

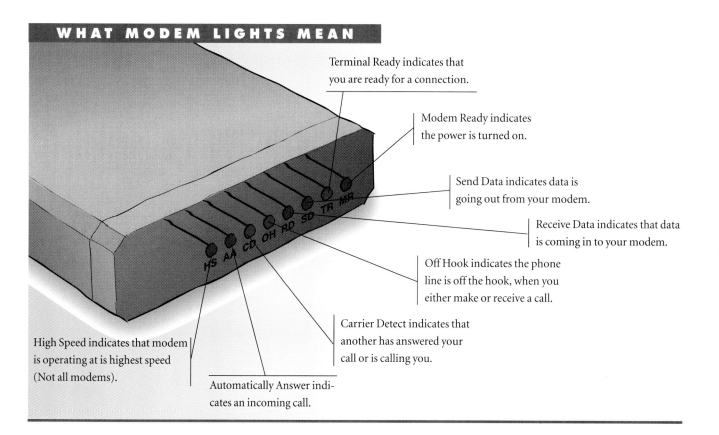

WHAT MODEM LIGHTS MEAN

Terminal Ready indicates that you are ready for a connection.

Modem Ready indicates the power is turned on.

Send Data indicates data is going out from your modem.

Receive Data indicates that data is coming in to your modem.

Off Hook indicates the phone line is off the hook, when you either make or receive a call.

Carrier Detect indicates that another has answered your call or is calling you.

High Speed indicates that modem is operating at is highest speed (Not all modems).

Automatically Answer indicates an incoming call.

into the modem port or the Apple Desktop Bus (ADB) port. When you use the Mac's ADB port, you won't need to connect an external power source as you will for modems that use the modem port. That's because the ADB port provides power to the modem, in addition to serving as the communications channel between the modem and the computer.

Once you've determined which serial port to use, the actual external modem installation is a piece of cake. But before you start, be sure that your computer is turned off. In fact, you should never connect any sort of cable to your computer while it is running. The rest of the installation is a simple matter of three basic connections: modem to computer, modem to phone jack, and modem to power source. The Installing an External Modem illustration describes what's involved.

NOTE *Even if you do have an extra phone jack, it's a good idea to connect your phone to your modem. Many modems prevent you from using the phone while the modem is using the*

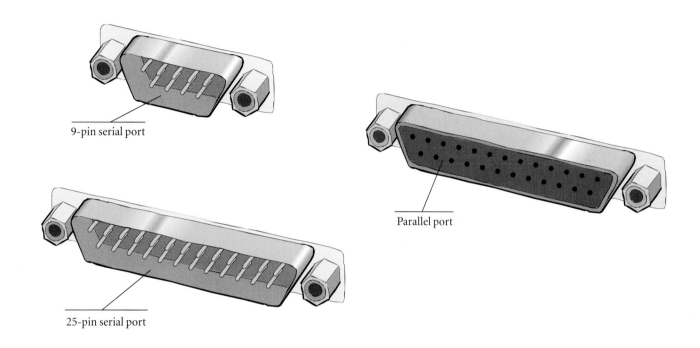

9-pin serial port

Parallel port

25-pin serial port

phone line. This prevents someone from picking up the phone and interrupting your com-

munications session. If you decide to connect your phone to your modem, you will be able to

use the phone even when the computer and modem are not turned on. And you'll get the

added benefit of having the computer dial the phone for you, should you wish to exploit the

auto-dial feature of some software programs. Auto-dial instructs the computer to dial a phone

number in your address database, for example.

INSTALLING AN INTERNAL MODEM

An internal modem is only slightly more difficult to install than an external one, but it takes a bit more courage for those who have never looked inside the guts of a computer. An internal modem plugs into a slot inside the computer; so before you buy an internal modem, make sure your computer has a slot to accommodate it. You can usually tell if there is an available slot without even taking the cover off the computer.

INSTALLING AN EXTERNAL MODEM

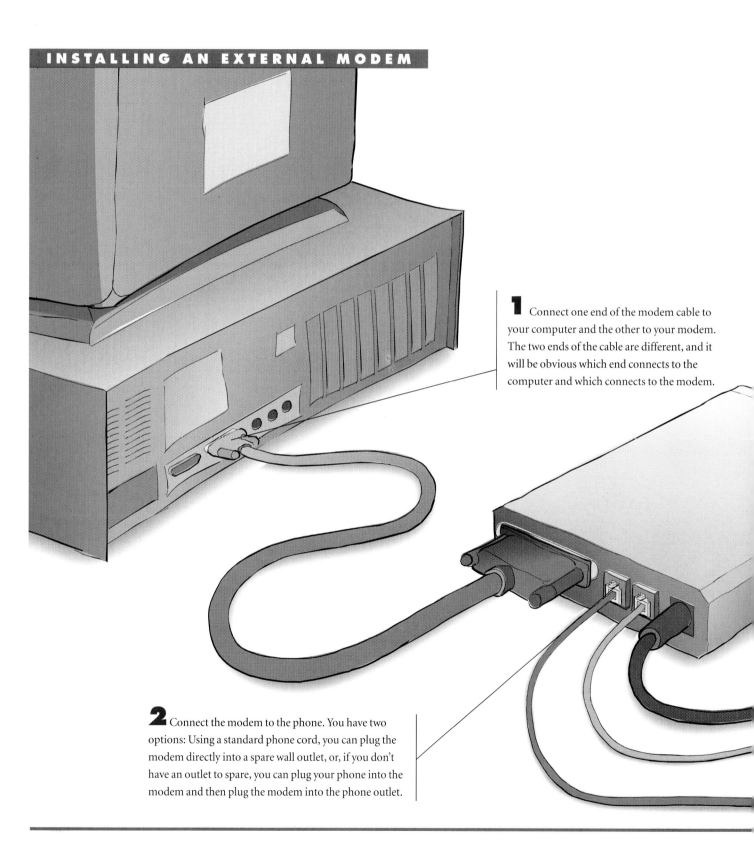

1 Connect one end of the modem cable to your computer and the other to your modem. The two ends of the cable are different, and it will be obvious which end connects to the computer and which connects to the modem.

2 Connect the modem to the phone. You have two options: Using a standard phone cord, you can plug the modem directly into a spare wall outlet, or, if you don't have an outlet to spare, you can plug your phone into the modem and then plug the modem into the phone outlet.

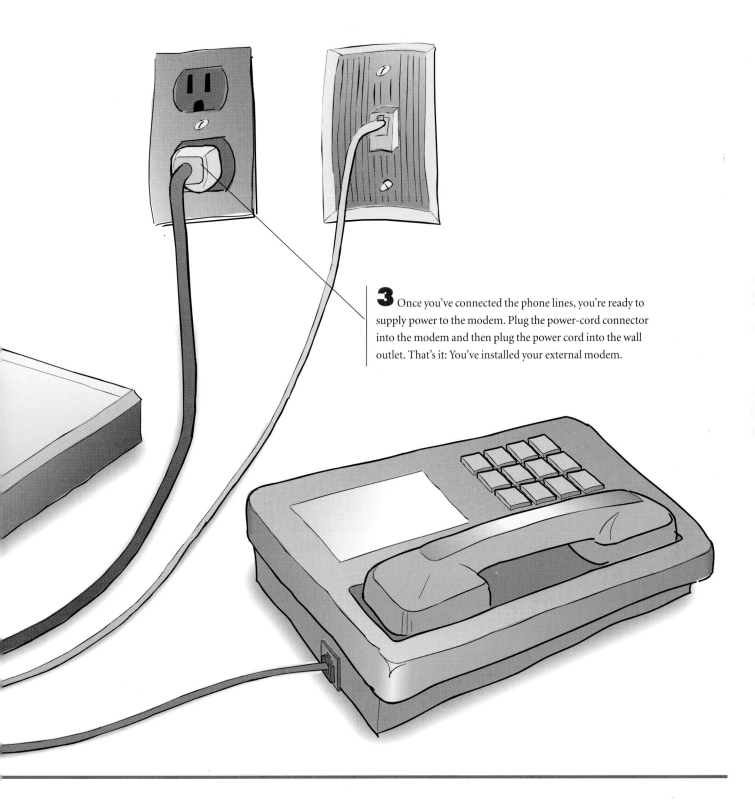

3 Once you've connected the phone lines, you're ready to supply power to the modem. Plug the power-cord connector into the modem and then plug the power cord into the wall outlet. That's it: You've installed your external modem.

Simply look at the back of the computer. You should see a row of two or more silver strips covering rectangular-shaped openings. Computer add-in cards have silver-colored metal end-brackets to hold them in place and to allow any external connectors to pass from the card to the outside of the computer. Computer manufacturers place fake end-brackets over the vacant slot openings to keep dust and other particles from entering the computer. You can differentiate between a fake end-bracket and one that is holding an add-in card in place in two ways. First, a connector on the bracket signifies a real add-in card. Second, if there are no connectors, tap the bracket with your finger. If it feels hollow, then there probably is no card attached to the bracket and the slot is available for use. Of course, the way to be absolutely sure if the slot is available is to take the cover off the computer and look inside.

As the name implies, a slot is simply a long, narrow opening on the computer's basic processing board (called a motherboard) that enables the add-in card to talk to the computer's microprocessor. IBM-compatible PCs have two types of slots: 8-bit and 16-bit. An 8-bit slot is a single receptacle, and a 16-bit slot consists of two receptacles placed end to end. Eight-bit slots send information from the processor to the add-in card 8 bits—or pieces—at a time, while 16-bit slots send information back and forth—you guessed it— 16 bits at a time. Most internal modems are 8-bit cards. You can install an 8-bit card in either an 8- or a 16-bit slot, but you can install a 16-bit card only in a 16-bit slot.

The illustration An Insider's View of a PC shows you what's under the hood after removing the cover from your computer.

Here's what you'll need to install an internal modem in a slot inside your computer: the internal modem card, a phone cord, and a screwdriver. It's very important to turn off your computer and unplug it from the wall outlet before installing an internal modem. This simple measure ensures that neither the computer nor you will suffer an electric shock. Electric shock can cause severe damage to computer components, not to mention the danger it poses to you. Never open your computer before turning it off and

AN INSIDER'S VIEW OF A PC

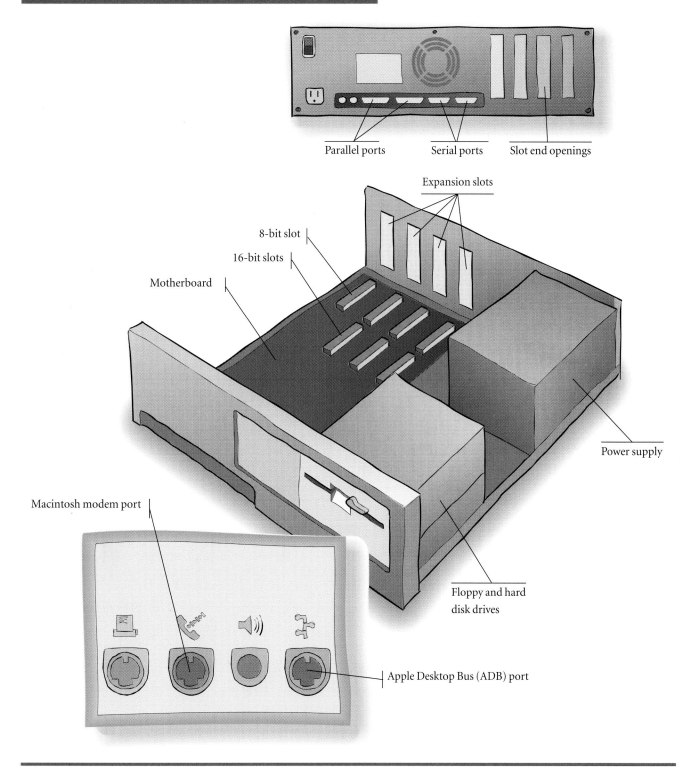

Parallel ports   Serial ports   Slot end openings

Expansion slots

8-bit slot

16-bit slots

Motherboard

Power supply

Macintosh modem port

Floppy and hard disk drives

Apple Desktop Bus (ADB) port

unplugging it from the wall. And discharge any static electricity by touching a piece of grounded metal, such as a light switch screw, before touching the computer. The illustration A Visual Guide to Installing an Internal Modem describes what's involved in the rest of the process.

NOTE *Internal modems and other add-in cards are delicate but not fragile. You can handle the modem and even bump it with some force without causing it to break. Don't be afraid to push as hard as necessary in order to fit the modem tightly into the slot. However, be sure that the connector is properly aligned with the slot receptacle before pressing down.*

INSTALLING COMMUNICATIONS SOFTWARE

You've installed your modem, but that by itself is no good. Without communications software, your modem can only sit inside or next to your computer and take up space. You need communications software to tell the modem what to do.

There are literally hundreds of communications software programs that all do basically the same thing: tell your modem to make or answer a call, give it the number to dial, and so on. In effect, the communications software is the boss and the modem does only what it is told to do. Some on-line services—such as America Online and the Prodigy Information Service—require that you use their own, unique communications software, which works only with those individual services. So you'll need to get a startup kit from these companies if you want to give their on-line services a try. Bulletin board systems and other on-line information services, such as CompuServe, can be reached using any standard communications package.

Installing communications software on either an IBM-compatible personal computer or a Macintosh involves two steps: copying the software onto your hard-disk drive and then setting up the software for use with your computer and modem. It would be impossible to give specific instructions on installing all the communications software you might choose to use, but there are some general procedures that will be common to all packages and I'll cover those here.

Installing PC Software Communications software for IBM-compatible computers comes in two flavors: those that run on DOS and those that run within the Microsoft Windows graphical operating environment. No matter which flavor, most communications packages will include an installation or setup program that handles the chore of copying the program onto your hard drive. Some will even take care of initial setup questions, such as whether you are using a color or monochrome monitor, what brand and speed of modem you have, and what COM port it is attached to. To launch the installation program of a DOS-based communications program, put the floppy disk in the appropriate disk drive (for this example, drive A). Next, follow these steps:

▶ *Be sure you are addressing the A drive by typing **A:** and pressing Enter. You should then see a prompt that looks like this: A:\>. Of course, if you are using the B drive to install your software, you'll need to type **B:** and press Enter. You should see the B:\> prompt.*

▶ *Check your communications software manual to find out what command you need to type at the A:\> prompt to start the installation program, or type **DIR** *****.EXE** and press Enter to get a listing of all program files on the floppy disk. Look for a file with a name such as INSTALL.EXE or SETUP.EXE. That's the program you need to start the installation process. (For this example, INSTALL.EXE is the program name.)*

▶ *Type **INSTALL** and press Enter at the A:\> prompt to start the installation program.*

INSTALLING AN INTERNAL MODEM

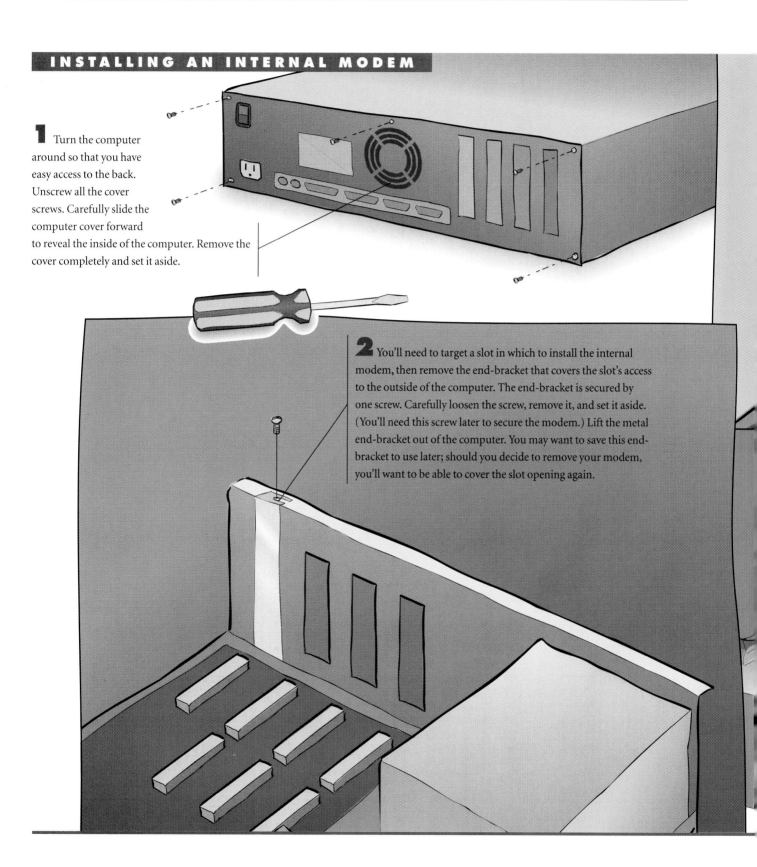

1 Turn the computer around so that you have easy access to the back. Unscrew all the cover screws. Carefully slide the computer cover forward to reveal the inside of the computer. Remove the cover completely and set it aside.

2 You'll need to target a slot in which to install the internal modem, then remove the end-bracket that covers the slot's access to the outside of the computer. The end-bracket is secured by one screw. Carefully loosen the screw, remove it, and set it aside. (You'll need this screw later to secure the modem.) Lift the metal end-bracket out of the computer. You may want to save this end-bracket to use later; should you decide to remove your modem, you'll want to be able to cover the slot opening again.

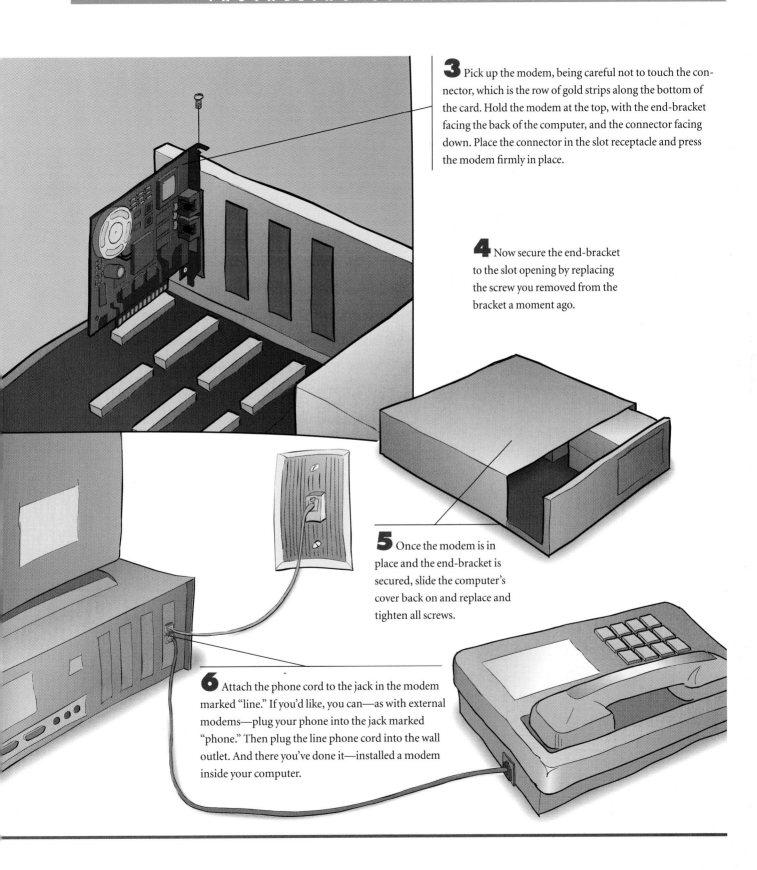

3 Pick up the modem, being careful not to touch the connector, which is the row of gold strips along the bottom of the card. Hold the modem at the top, with the end-bracket facing the back of the computer, and the connector facing down. Place the connector in the slot receptacle and press the modem firmly in place.

4 Now secure the end-bracket to the slot opening by replacing the screw you removed from the bracket a moment ago.

5 Once the modem is in place and the end-bracket is secured, slide the computer's cover back on and replace and tighten all screws.

6 Attach the phone cord to the jack in the modem marked "line." If you'd like, you can—as with external modems—plug your phone into the jack marked "phone." Then plug the line phone cord into the wall outlet. And there you've done it—installed a modem inside your computer.

▶ *The installation program will likely ask you a few questions, such as where you'd like to install the software (the default answer provided by the program is usually the best thing for you to choose), the type of modem you have, how fast it is, and so on. Simply answer the questions as they appear and the software installation program does the rest.*

▶ *Once the installation program has successfully completed its task, you are ready to start up the communications software. The installation program may do this for you, or it may leave a message on screen telling you what command to enter in order to start the program. If it does neither of these, consult your manual or, if necessary, change directories to the directory where the program was installed and type DIR *.EXE at the prompt. You'll get a list of program files (probably a very short list), and the one that is similar to the software's name is likely the command you type to launch the program.*

If the DOS-based communications software you choose doesn't have an installation program, copy the program from the floppy disk(s) to a new directory on your hard drive. To do this, first make a directory to hold the communications software files. At the C:\ prompt, type **MD \COMM** and press Enter. This tells the PC to make a directory called COMM. (You can call this directory anything you'd like, perhaps the name of the program itself. I'll just use COMM here as an example.) Then copy all the files from the floppy disk(s) in drive A, for example, into the new directory by typing **COPY *.*** **C:\COMM** at the A:> prompt. After you've copied the files to your hard drive, type **DIR *.EXE** at the C:\COMM prompt to find the program file name that will launch the program. The file name that most resembles the name of the program you are using is likely the command you'll type to get things started.

To install a Windows-based communications package, place the program disk in drive A, for example. Then choose Run from the File menu of the Windows Program

Manager. A dialog box asks you what program you would like to run. Type **A:** and the file name of the installation program, usually INSTALL or SETUP. If you're not sure which file name to use, check your software manual or use the Browse button in the Run dialog box to find the appropriate executable file on the disk in drive A. (An executable file is the same as a program file and is denoted by the file extension .EXE, or sometimes .BAT.)

Installing Mac Software   The Macintosh desktop makes installing new software a bit easier than it is on an IBM-compatible PC. You can install many Mac programs by simply copying the program from the floppy disk to the hard disk. To do this, put the floppy disk in the disk drive. A floppy-disk icon appears in the upper-right corner of your screen, with a label name—for example, Communications—given to it by the communications software developer. Select the floppy-disk icon by moving the mouse pointer over the icon and clicking the mouse button and holding it down. Still holding the mouse button down, drag the floppy-disk icon and place it over the Macintosh HD (hard disk) icon. Release the mouse button and the Mac copies the floppy-disk files onto the hard disk. Later, you can find the contents of the floppy disk in a folder that has the same name as the floppy disk (in this example, the folder would be named Communications).

Some more complex Macintosh programs, typically those that come on two or more floppy disks, have an installation program that does the copying and tells you when it is done with one floppy disk and ready to copy the next. To install these programs to your Mac hard drive, place the first disk into the floppy-disk drive. When the floppy-disk icon appears in the upper-right corner, move your mouse cursor to the icon and click the mouse button. The contents of the floppy disk appear on screen. Find the program icon that indicates the installation program, and click on that icon. This launches the installation program, which will walk you through the process of copying files, swapping floppy disks, and the like through a series of messages on the screen. Just follow those directions and your communications software will be ready to use in no time.

NOTE *The Macintosh allows you to run programs automatically when you start up the computer by placing file icons in the Mac's Startup Items folder. These programs are launched each time your turn on your computer. Before installing Mac software, it's a good idea to restart your Macintosh without launching the programs in the Startup Items folder. To do this on Macs running System 7, simply hold down the Shift key when you turn on the computer.*

CONFIGURING YOUR SOFTWARE

Now that your software is installed and running, you need to get it ready for work. Whether you are using a PC or a Macintosh, you must specify a number of communications settings so that the software will work successfully with the modem and with the bulletin board or on-line service you are trying to call. Depending on the software you use, you may have to set your communications settings in two places: one place for general settings, such as the COM port, that apply to all your connections, and another place for settings specific to the bulletin board or service you are trying to call. Each bulletin board and on-line service works slightly differently and requires different communications settings, but it's most likely that you will specify the settings for each phone number you enter in the program's dialing directory.

Deep in the bowels of most communications software there are lots of techie tweaks and switches, and someday you may want to adventure into them. But for now, these are the most common settings you'll need to understand in order to configure your communications software:

▶ *COM Port   This setting tells the software where to look to find the modem. The default setting—that is, the setting the software assumes is correct—is usually COM1. If you have installed your modem on another COM port, say COM2, you'll want to change the default setting accordingly.*

▶ *Modem Speed or Baud Rate   Usually you will want to specify the fastest speed at which your modem can communicate. However, some bulletin boards, on-line* services, and electronic mail services operate at a variety of speeds and use specific telephone numbers depending on the speed of the modem that will be answering your call. If you don't know the speed of the modem you are calling, go ahead and specify the fastest speed of your modem. Most often, your modem will be smart enough to slow down and talk at the speed of the modem at the other end.

▶ *Parity*   In a nutshell, parity is the way the communications software checks the data it receives to ensure that it is, in fact, the data that was supposed to be sent. Most often, set parity to "none" unless you know for certain it should be at another setting.

▶ *Data Bits*   This setting tells the modem how many binary characters (the 1s and 0s that computers use to represent numbers and text) will be used to represent one character of information. The default setting is usually 8. Use this setting unless you know it ought to be set differently.

▶ *Stop Bits*   This setting tells the modem how many binary characters are used between the data bit streams to indicate a complete character has been sent. In essence, it is the pause between characters. Set stop bits to 1, unless you know it should be set to another value.

▶ *Duplex*   Sometimes, data flows both to and from the modem at the same time. This is called full duplex. Other times, data must be sent and received in turn. This is called half duplex. Unless you know the setting should be half duplex, use full duplex as the default.

▶ *Protocol*   This is the method by which files are transferred from one computer to another. The protocol indicates what information is received and checks the information for accuracy. In order for two computers to exchange files, they must use the same protocol, and there are a dozen or so common protocols from which to choose. Typically you can make this choice when the time comes to send a file to or

CONFIGURING YOUR COMMUNICATIONS SOFTWARE

This illustration shows the Dialing Menu in Procomm Plus and its communications settings.

Parity setting options:
NONE
EVEN
Modem speed for this   ODD
phone number   MARK   Data bits and stop bits
SPACE

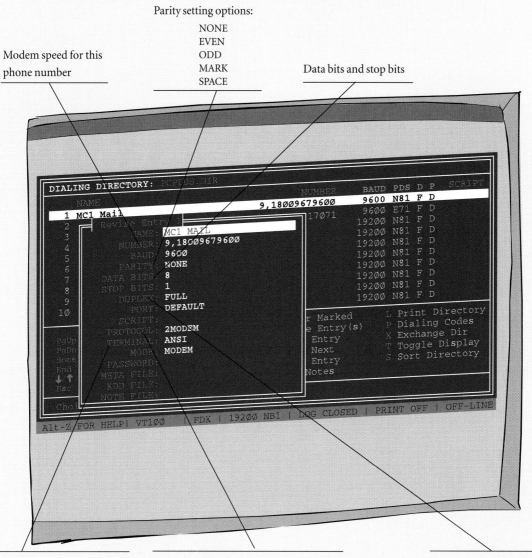

Terminal setting options:

IBM PC
ANSI
WYSE
VT100
IBM 3101
3270/E50

and dozens more. ANSI works in most cases
where terminal setting is not specified.

Protocol setting options:

XModem
ZModem
YModem
COMPUSERVE B+
KERMIT
ASCII

and nearly a dozen more. ZModem is a good choice
where the protocol setting is not otherwise specified.

Duplex setting options:

FULL
HALF

receive a file from another computer. You can save a step by specifying a default protocol in your software setup. A widely supported protocol is ZModem.

▶ *Terminal   Because your computer typically goes "dumb" (it's simply sending and receiving information, not processing it) when it's communicating with another, usually bigger computer, you must specify the type of terminal you want your computer to appear to be. Usually, your software will give you a list of terminal types from which to choose. Pick the default setting, if there is one, or choose one of the "plain vanilla" terminal emulations, such as ANSI or VT100.*

THE AT COMMAND SET

Communications software talks to your modem through a standard language known as the AT (pronounced *a-tee*) command set. The AT command set—a series of instructions that tell the modem what to do and how to do it—was developed by Hayes Microcomputer Products as a way to allow software to direct modems as necessary, rather than relying only on the preprogrammed instructions embedded in the modem hardware. Hayes modems became so popular that the AT command set has been adopted by virtually every PC modem manufacturer. The AT commands are a means of getting the modem's attention and then issuing an instruction, such as dial a touch-tone phone (ATDT) or hang up the phone line (ATH). There are dozens of AT commands. Blissfully, all but the most arcane communications software interpret your plain English instruction (dial the phone number 555-1111) into AT commands that the modem understands (ATDT #5551111). You needn't learn these commands or even pay them much attention at all. But you will want a general understanding of what the AT command set is so that you'll be in the know when your software flashes AT command strings on your screen. If you do want to delve more deeply into these commands and how to use them to control your modem's features, consult the index of your communications software or modem manual.

Once you've established your default communications settings, you're just about ready to make your first connection. The only thing left is to tell the software which phone number you'd like it to dial.

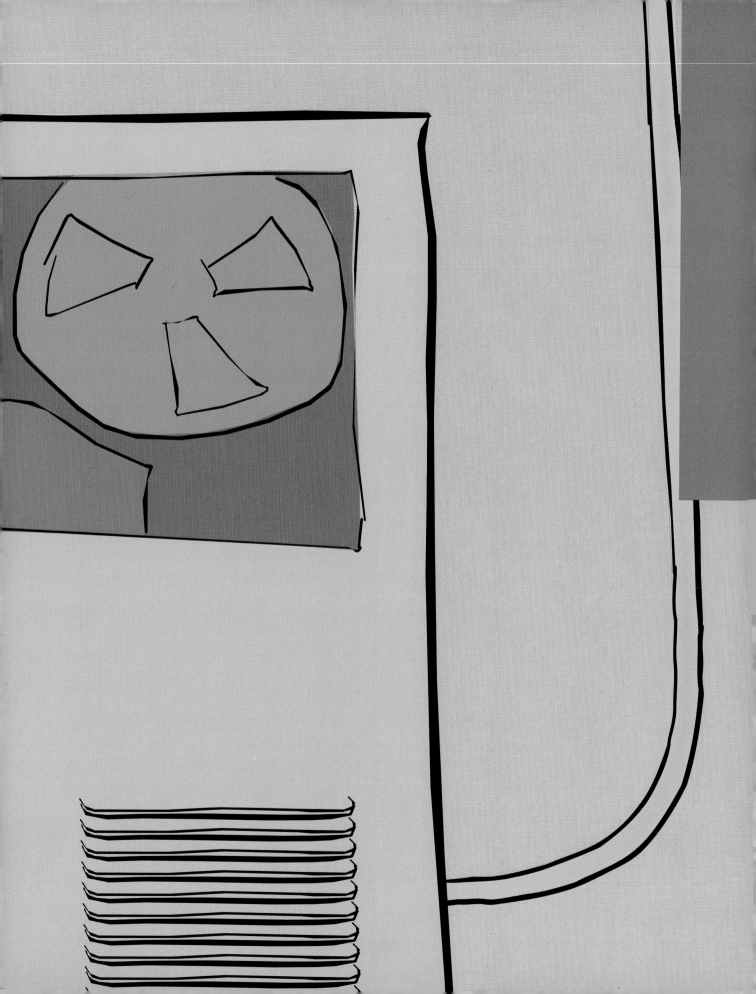

MAKING YOUR FIRST CONNECTION

Kinds of Connections

■

Establishing a Connection

■

Breaking a Connection

■

What to Do If Something Goes Wrong

Learning the information in Chapters 1 through 5 has been for you like

warm-up exercises are for an athlete. It has strengthened your understanding of connecting, stretched your imagination, and made you ready for the main event— making your first connection. Now you know what you can do on line, how people interact when they are on line, and the cultural norms and secret language they use. You have the equipment to make a connection and you've got your communications software installed, configured, and running. Now that you're ready to go, well, just what kinds of connections can you make?

KINDS OF CONNECTIONS

Basically, there are three kinds of PC connections:

▶ *Direct connection between PCs*

▶ *Connection to a mainframe computer*

▶ *Connection to an on-line service*

In one way, all these connections are similar. They are all *serial connections*. Serial simply means that bits of data are transmitted across the connection one after another in a series. (This is in contrast to parallel connections, most often used to connect a PC and a printer. In parallel connections, several bits of data are transmitted as a group across the connection.) Just as you might expect, serial connections are made through the PC's serial port, while parallel connections occur through the parallel port.

But while all of the three types of connections are similar, they are also different. This section briefly explains each of these connections and how you might use them at work or at home. Throughout this chapter, I'll refer to the computer at the other end of the connection as the *remote computer*.

Connecting to Another PC   One PC can "call" another PC just like one phone "calls" another—modems at both ends of the connection talk to one another. In the most basic PC-to-PC connection, one PC acts as the sender of information and the other acts as the receiver. In the course of the connection, the roles can reverse: The recipient can become the sender and vice versa. Typically, you would use a PC-to-PC connection to send a document or a program file to someone else, without going through an intermediate electronic mail service. You begin by simply dialing the remote PC. The modem—with the help of the communications software—answers the call. Now, both PCs are able to talk to one another. The person at one end of the connection can send a file to the computer at the other end of the connection by selecting the software command to send a file and telling the communication software which file to send. The person at the receiving end selects the software command that enables his or her PC to receive the incoming file. Then both parties sit back as the file is transferred from one PC to the other.

A second kind of PC-to-PC connection lets you call a remote computer and take control of that computer's operation, just as if you were sitting at that computer's keyboard. This is known as remote-control access and requires communications software, such as Symantec's PC/Anywhere, specifically designed to do this task. A remote connection is handy when you need to get information from another computer, say, the PC you have at work, when you are away from it. Using your PC at home, for example, you can call your work computer, copy files from the work PC to your home PC, delete files, and create new ones. The PC at the other end of the connection gives you full access to its hard disk; you can run any DOS command on the remote computer just as if you were sitting at its keyboard. You can even launch and use any application installed on the remote PC. The one real drawback to this kind of remote computing is that it can be very tedious and slow. Every keystroke you enter has to be sent to the other PC, it responds, and sends you a duplicate image of its screen back across the phone line.

THE THREE CONNECTIONS

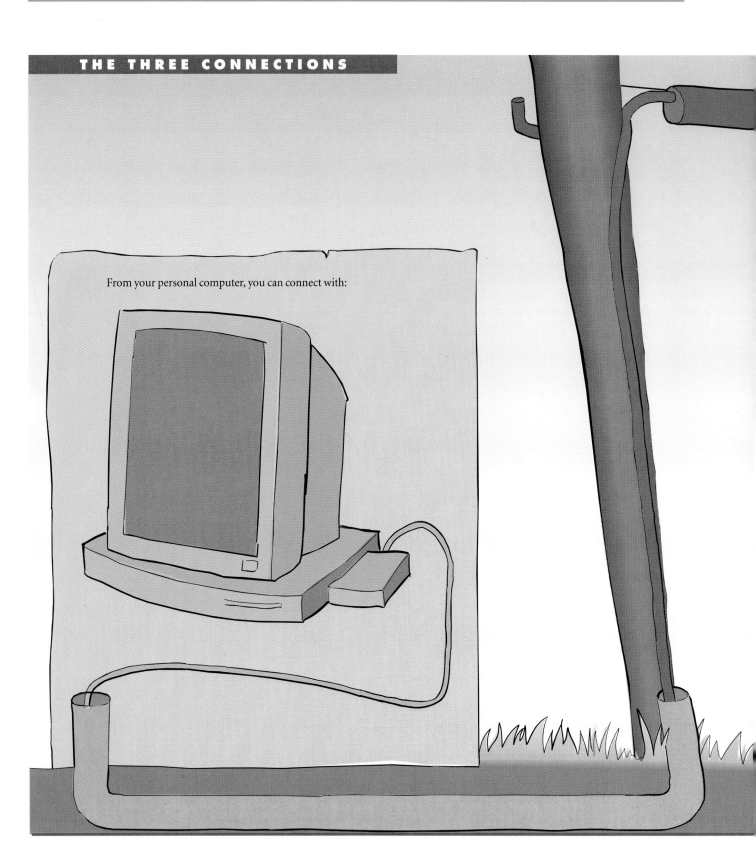

From your personal computer, you can connect with:

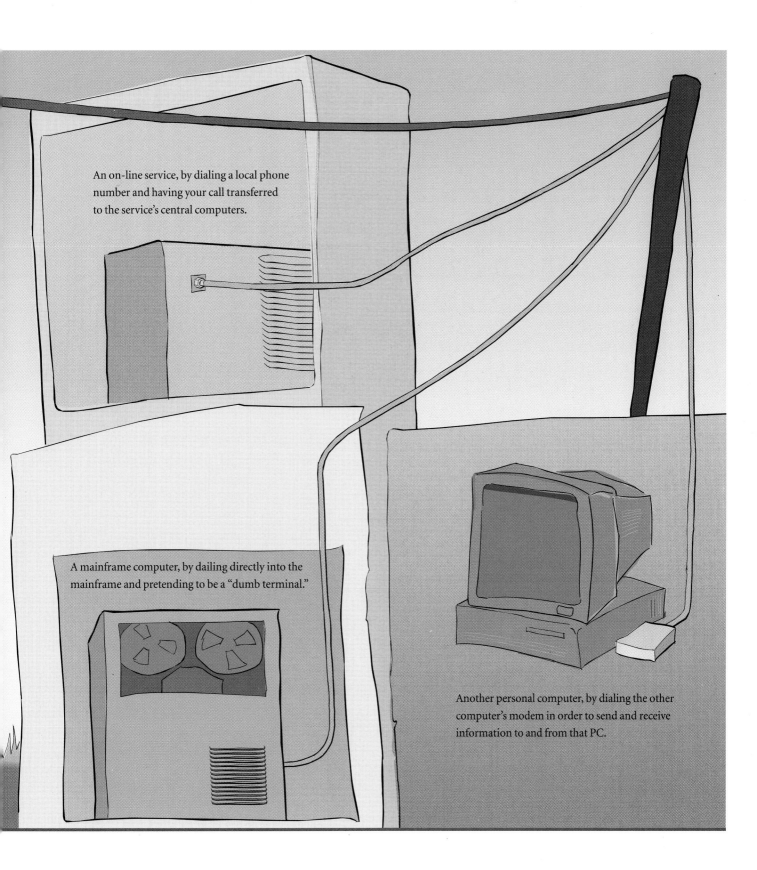

An on-line service, by dialing a local phone number and having your call transferred to the service's central computers.

A mainframe computer, by dailing directly into the mainframe and pretending to be a "dumb terminal."

Another personal computer, by dialing the other computer's modem in order to send and receive information to and from that PC.

N O T E   *Most all remote-control access software includes security provisions to ensure that unwanted intruders can't gain access to the remote computer. A simple password will provide enough protection for most applications, but you may want to consider a remote-control access program that includes "call-back" protection for highly sensitive uses. Call-back protection is just what it sounds like: You call the remote computer and tell the computer who you are. The remote computer hangs up the connection and calls back your computer at a specified, predetermined phone number. You answer the call, tell the computer who you are, and enter your password. This way, you can access the remote computer only if you are an authorized user, have a valid password, and are calling from a specific phone number.*

Connecting to a Mainframe Computer   You may have heard the phrase "micro-to-mainframe link" to describe the connection between a personal computer and a mainframe or a minicomputer. In this kind of connection, the PC connects to a mainframe computer as a *dumb terminal*. A dumb terminal is essentially a keyboard and screen hooked up to a mainframe computer. Mainframe computer operators use dumb terminals to send instructions and information to the mainframe and to see the results of their instructions. Mainframe terminals are considered "dumb" because, unlike PCs, they don't have the ability to process information independently of the mainframe computer. PCs talk to mainframes by using the terminal emulation mode found in communications software. If you use your PC to dial into the mainframe computer at your work, then you've established a micro-to-mainframe link.

Connecting to an On-line Service   Connecting to an on-line service is not unlike a micro-to-mainframe connection. But there's a twist. On-line services usually consist of one or more central computers linked by telephone lines to other smaller computers peppered across the country. When you call an on-line service, you are actually calling a local computer. If the local computer has the information you want, it sends it to you directly. If not, it turns to the central computer to fetch the information you request.

ESTABLISHING A CONNECTION

Your communications software is the command center for all your connections. Through it, you direct the modem to dial the phone number of another computer and then connect to this remote computer. The software allows you to see the messages the remote computer sends to you. You can then answer the remote computer's requests for information, instruct the remote computer to show you specific information, send information to be saved on your computer, or let it know what information you are sending to it.

Every communications program works differently, but the main concepts of connecting remain constant from program to program. For the purposes of this chapter, I'll use a very popular Windows-based program called Procomm Plus for Windows to illustrate how to make a connection. The concepts and the terminology used with this communications software are similar to those for all other communications packages, but you may need to poke around in your software's menus to find the equivalents to the commands mentioned here. If you have any trouble, consult your software manual for more specific guidance. You may also want to refer to the section that covers communications software in Chapter 5 of this book.

A small bulletin board operated by the Boston Computer Society is the recipient of the example call. I've chosen this bulletin board because it is representative of the bulletin board systems that are available to most computer users through a local phone call. Moreover, the procedures for connecting to a major on-line service, such as CompuServe, are not significantly different from dialing into a bulletin board of this type.

Before you can make a connection, you've got to launch your communications software. If you are using a DOS-based communications program, consult your manual to find out what command to type at the DOS prompt. Often, the command is some variation of the name of the program. For example, the DOS version of Procomm Plus includes a file called PCPLUS.EXE. You type **PCPLUS** at the DOS prompt to launch this program. You can also figure out how to launch the program by looking in the directory in which your communications software is installed. You may need to change between hard-disk directories to the one where the program is installed. To do this, type **CD**, a space, the name of the directory, and press Enter. Then you'll need to type the command to launch your program. To determine the command, type **DIR *.EXE** at the DOS prompt. You'll see a short list of file names. The file name that is most similar to the name of the communications software you are using is probably the command to type to start the program. Once you know the command, type it at the DOS prompt to launch the program.

N O T E *DOS commands are not* case sensitive, *meaning you can type them in either upper- or lowercase and they'll work just fine.*

If you are using Windows or Mac software, find the communications program icon in the Windows Program Manager or the Mac desktop. Move your mouse cursor over the icon, and click the mouse button twice to initiate the program.

Once you have the communications software running, take a few minutes to explore its menus. Specifically, look for menu items that indicate a phone book or other place where you'll keep a list of the on-line services you will call. Find the commands that dial the modem and that end the connection. If your communications software has a tutorial, take the time to run it. This will give you the best overview of the particular features of your software. If there's no tutorial, take a moment to explore the program's help menu. Often, you can find answers to your questions even before you know to ask them.

Entering the Calling Information Now that you've become familiar with your communications program, you need to give it the information necessary for it to make the first call. Most communications programs have some sort of phone list where you enter the name, phone number, and specific information for the connection you want to make. Procomm Plus for Windows refers to this list as the dialing directory, other

LAUNCHING YOUR SOFTWARE

If you're using a DOS-based communications program, consult your manual to find out what command to type at the DOS prompt. Often, the command is some variation of the name of the program. For example, the DOS version of Procomm Plus includes a file called PCPLUS.EXE. You type **PCPLUS** at the DOS prompt to launch this program.

C:\PCPLUS\PCPLUS.EXE

programs may call it a phone book or a phone log, or simply settings, as in the case of the Windows Terminal program. Whatever it's called in the software you are using, find the command—probably called new entry, phone number, or something similar—that provides a place to enter information about the connection.

No matter what bulletin board or on-line service you call, you'll need to enter some information about the service in order to make an effective connection. Typically, all this information will be entered on the same screen. Of course, the first thing to enter is the name of the service and its phone number. Enter the phone number just as you would if you were dialing it on the phone. If you're calling from an office phone system that requires you dial a 9, for example, to reach an outside line, remember to enter a 9 at the beginning of the phone number. If the number is a long-distance call, remember to enter a 1, too. You will want to enter a comma after the 9 to tell the modem to pause a minute while the phone service makes the proper connections. And while you would type dashes between the area code, prefix, and number if you were including the phone number in a document, for example, you don't have to include the dashes in your communications software's phone directory. So, for example, if you were calling the Boston Computer Society's bulletin board from an office phone system, your phone-number entry might look like this:

`9,16179657046`

After you've entered the phone number, you'll need to tell the software what modem speed to use when you call this particular number. Most bulletin boards and on-line services list the modem speeds they can accommodate or provide a specific phone number for each modem speed. If you can find no such mention for the service you want to call, enter the fastest speed of your modem. When the modem connects to the service, it will slow down if it finds a modem of a lower speed at the other end of the connection. The section What to Look for in a Modem, in Chapter 4, discusses modem speeds.

Now comes the tricky part. You need to tell the software what communications settings to use when it connects with this service. These settings include data bits; stop bits; none, even, or odd parity; and full or half duplex. This is tricky only because often you won't know what settings the remote computer requires, so you may have to do a little trial and error to get the correct settings. In most cases, you'll be okay if you set data bits to 8, stop bits to 1, parity to none, and duplex to full, unless you have specific instructions otherwise. If communications settings are not correct, you will get strings of nonsense characters on screen when you make your connection. When this happens, hang up and adjust your data bits. Try setting data bits to 7, stop bits to 1, and parity to even. Then call the service again. In most cases, this will solve the problem and the characters on screen will come across in understandable English. You may want to refer to Configuring Your Software, in Chapter 5.

Making a Call   Now that you've told the software what phone number to call, it's time to go on line. Use the communications software's dial command to have the modem dial the service number. In most communications programs, you simply highlight the phone number in the phone directory and press Enter or select a dial command from a menu, or, as in the case of Procomm Plus for Windows, click on a dial button in the dialing directory. You should hear a dial tone through your modem, then a series of tones as the number is being dialed.

In most cases, when a modem answers a call, your software will place a message on screen telling you that you are connected to another computer. The software may even beep to be sure it gets your attention. When I call the Boston Computer Society bulletin board using Procomm Plus for Windows, for example, the software flashes a message at the bottom left of the screen that says "CONNECT 9600 to Boston Computer Society." Procomm Plus gets this information from the modem speed I've specified and from the name associated with the phone number in the dialing directory. When the *connect message* appears, press the Enter key once or twice. This signals to the remote computer that you're there and ready to go.

You're On Line! Now What?   Once your modem has connected to a remote computer and you've pressed the Enter key once or twice to tell the remote computer you're there, the rest of the connection is essentially a matter of follow the leader. The remote computer asks you a question and you answer it. By following the computer's instructions, you can register with the service and begin to explore.

The first time you dial into a bulletin board or on-line service, you'll be asked a number of questions—such as your name, the city in which you live, and daytime phone number. The service operators will use this information if you've forgotten your password (discussed next) and the service must confirm that you are indeed who you say you are when you call asking to be allowed back onto the service. Moreover, by asking for

SETTING UP A CALL

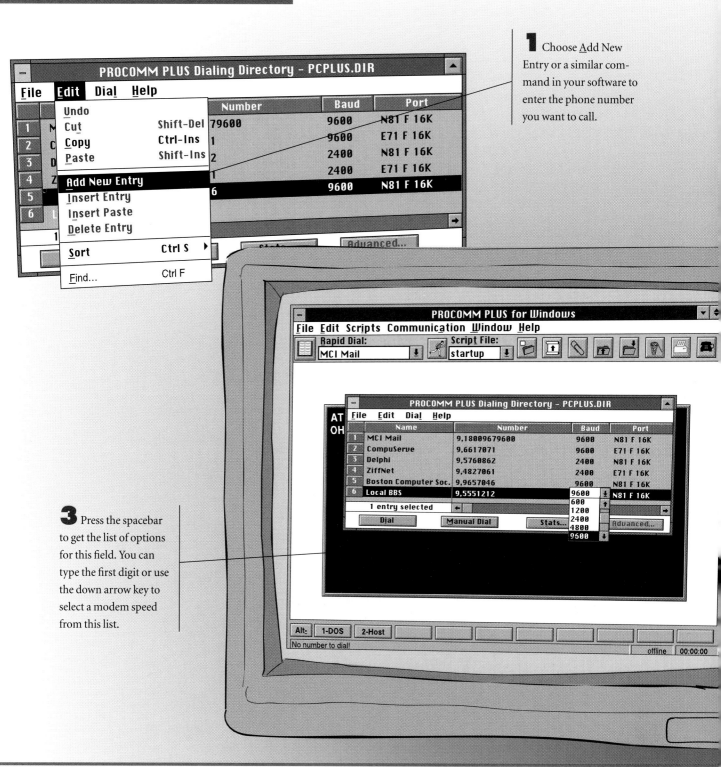

1 Choose <u>A</u>dd New Entry or a similar command in your software to enter the phone number you want to call.

3 Press the spacebar to get the list of options for this field. You can type the first digit or use the down arrow key to select a modem speed from this list.

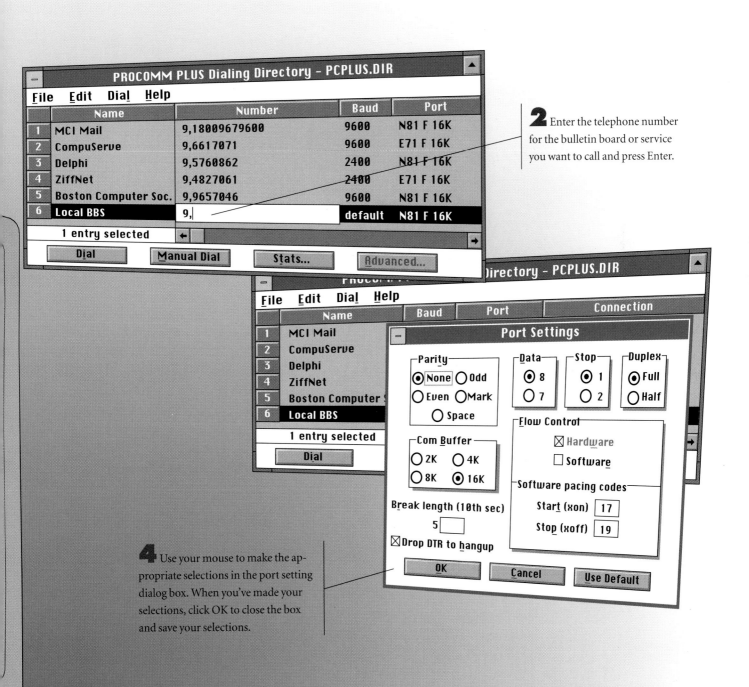

2 Enter the telephone number for the bulletin board or service you want to call and press Enter.

4 Use your mouse to make the appropriate selections in the port setting dialog box. When you've made your selections, click OK to close the box and save your selections.

DIALING A BULLETIN BOARD

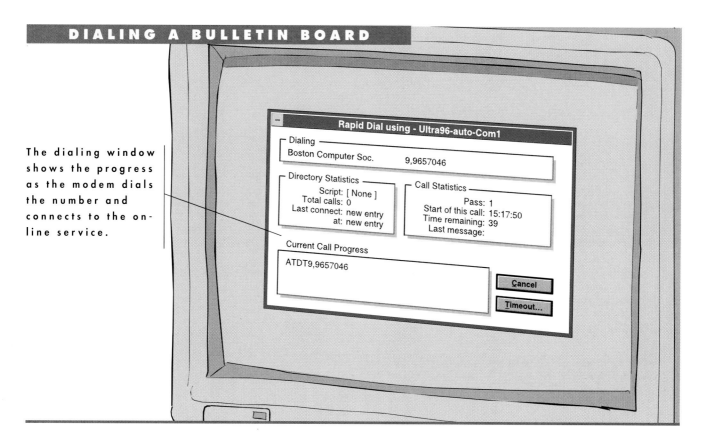

The dialing window shows the progress as the modem dials the number and connects to the on-line service.

your phone number, the bulletin board operator is checking, in a sense, that those calling the bulletin board are serious users, even if they only want to use the bulletin board once. When you have to ante up your phone number, you think twice about fooling around. The on-line service will also ask you to choose a password and type it at the prompt. Then you will be asked to type the password again to confirm that what you typed the first time is indeed what you thought you typed. If you're calling a commercial on-line service for the first time, the remote computer will ask you to enroll in the service and will request billing information, including your address and most likely a credit card number. Commercial on-line services will follow up on these on-line membership enrollments with a mailing that includes a welcome letter and a user guide.

For subsequent connections, the first thing the remote computer will ask is your name and password. This is called *logging on* to the service. The log on procedure for an on-line service is much like some office building security procedures. The first time you enter a building where you will work, a security guard asks some questions, has you sign in, and issues a security pass. On subsequent visits, you might only have to show the pass in order to enter the building. It's similar with on-line services. Your password is the gate key to any on-line service you might join. You must have the password in order to gain access to the service. And just as you wouldn't leave your house keys lying around for anyone to borrow, you don't want to make your password available for others to use. (You might be surprised how many people write passwords on Post-It Notes attached to their monitors.) By the same token, you will want to choose a password that is not too obvious. Avoid the word "password," your name, birth date, or other personal information that others might easily know about you. In other words, make it virtually impossible for others to figure out your password and log on to the service as if they were you. This not only prevents a scofflaw from sailing through the service disguised as you, more importantly, it also keeps the culprit from running up your on-line service bill.

NOTE *While you want to make your password hard for others to figure out, you want to make it easy for you to remember. If you do forget your password, however, contact the bulletin board or on-line service by phone. You'll have to answer some questions to prove you are who you say you are, then the service will tell you your password. It's a good idea, then, to log on to the service and change your password to something easier to remember.*

After you've entered your name and password, you are free to roam about the bulletin board or on-line service, getting acquainted with its commands and exploring the information it offers. This roaming is often referred to as *navigating* the on-line service because, in effect, you are sailing through a sea of information and must navigate from port to port in order to get the information you most want. In one way or another on-line services provide a menu of navigation options. The Boston Computer Society bulletin board's approach is a common one. It provides a menu of commands whenever you need to make a choice. You choose the command by selecting the uppercase letter in the

LOGGING ON TO A BULLETIN BOARD

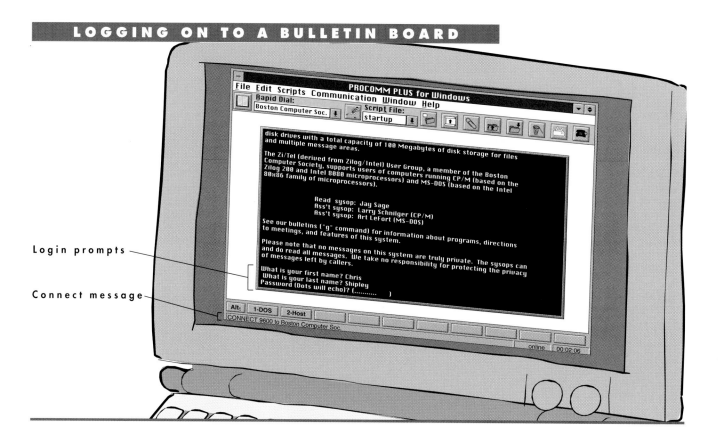

Login prompts

Connect message

menu listing. For example, some commands are R to Read bulletin board messages, F to get a list of downloadable Files, and H to access system Help. In addition to these menus, on-line services welcome callers with a message about what's new on the service. These messages, often called *highlights*, either provide menu choices to take you directly to some specific information, or they provide instructions on how to navigate to the information discussed in the message.

NOTE *Each on-line service has its own navigational methods. CompuServe, for example, uses "go" words that you type at the service prompt in order to reach different information areas of the service. If you type **GO TOUR** at the prompt, for example, CompuServe takes you on a guided tour of its features. Similarly, America Online has a Go To command, which you use in combination with keywords to move through the service. Selecting Go To Hotline takes you to America Online's customer relations hotline. The Prodigy Information Service* *uses "jump" words to move from section to section. JUMP MEMBER SERVICES is the command to get answers to your questions about Prodigy. You'll learn much more about how to navigate these and other on-line information services in Chapter 9.*

One of the first places to investigate after you log on to a bulletin board or on-line service is the message area, where members post notes to one another. These message sections of a bulletin board or on-line service, more than almost anything else, reveal the character of the on-line service. It is here that members let their hair down and speak their minds, no matter if the topic is the best word processing software or the best chili recipe. As you read through these messages, you can imagine that you've walked through the doors of a private club and you are able to overhear club members' conversations. If the topics and the tone of the conversations appeal to you, then join the club and join in the conversation. If not, hang up and try another service.

BREAKING A CONNECTION

Once you've had a look around the on-line service and gotten a feel for what it offers, you're ready to break the connection—at least for now. Hanging up is easy, but just as some methods of ending a telephone conversation are more graceful than others, there are graceful and not-so-graceful ways to end an on-line connection. If you're using an external modem, you can bring any connection to an abrupt conclusion by turning off the power to the modem or shutting off the computer. But it's better to use the hang-up option in your communications software to disconnect the call and reset the modem for the next connection. Best of all, of course, is to tell the on-line connection that you're leaving. Each system has at least one way to say good-bye. The Boston Computer Society bulletin board, like many other bulletin board services, uses the command G for good-bye. Both exit and bye will work on CompuServe. The Prodigy menu has an END selection to disconnect you from the service. And exit works for MCI Mail.

N O T E   *Generally, on-line navigational commands are not case sensitive. You can type* ***exit, EXIT, Exit, eXiT,*** *or any other combination of upper- and lowercase characters and still get the same effect.*

No matter which prompt you use, the act of saying so long to the on-line service is called logging off. It's always a good idea to log off when you are through using the service so that the service knows that you have completed your transactions naturally, rather than being cut off by some quirk of the phone system, for example. Without the formal log off, the system will wait for some amount of time to be sure you are no longer at the other end of the connection. Logging off frees the system to take a call from another user and—especially important for services that bill you for the time you use—alerts the system to stop the timer on your account.

Although the example I've used in this chapter is specific to Procomm Plus for Windows, the general steps for making a connection will be the same no matter which program you use.

WHAT TO DO IF SOMETHING GOES WRONG

Most on-line connections will go quite smoothly, but there are a few common error messages that you may run into from time to time. When you try to dial the modem, you may get a "no dial tone" message. Be sure that the modem is connected to the phone cord and the phone cord is connected to the wall jack. If the modem dials the number and gets a busy signal, you'll get a "line busy" message. Just hang up the modem and try again later. And sometimes when you are on line your connection is interrupted for any number of reasons. You'll likely get a message that says something like "carrier lost." Simply dial the number and start again.

LOGGING OFF AND HANGING UP

Once you've logged off the service, select the hang up command from the communications software's menu. This will tell the communications software to cut the phone connection and get the modem ready for the next call.

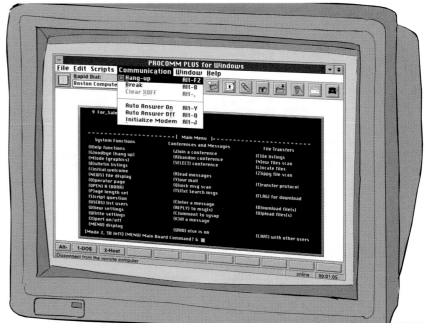

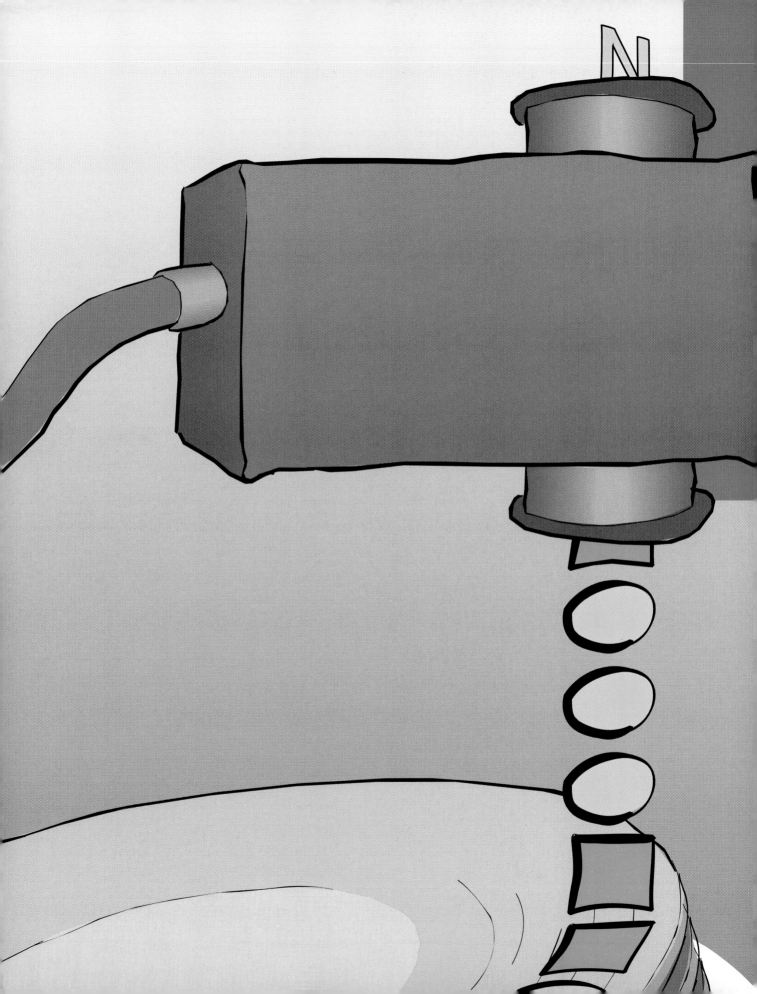

7

SENDING AND RECEIVING FILES

Kinds of Files You Can Transfer

■

File Transfer Protocols

■

Downloading a File

■

Sending Text and Binary Files

■

Compressing and Decompressing Files

Dig around in any on-line source for just a few minutes, and you'll find applications programs—such as word processors, spreadsheets, and communications software—that are as useful as many of the programs you'd find in a software store. You'll also uncover interesting clip art, fonts, macros, and templates that you can use with the programs you already have. On-line services are rife with utility programs that handle important computer maintenance chores. And you can't help but find literally thousands of games of all varieties, from brain-teasing strategy games to shoot-'em-up arcade adventures. This chapter shows you how to capture these files for use on your computer.

On-line services and bulletin board systems (covered in Chapters 8 and 9, respectively) are a treasure trove of data and programs that you can copy to your computer. To copy these files to your computer, you must *download* them, an idea mentioned briefly in the first three chapters of this book. Downloading is simply the act of receiving a file from another computer, most often via an on-line service or a bulletin board system. Conversely, *uploading* is the act of sending a file to another computer. You might also hear the term *file transfer* to refer to both downloading and uploading. No matter what you call it, the process is an easy way to expand your computing horizons and a useful way to share information with others.

KINDS OF FILES YOU CAN TRANSFER

Essentially, there are two kinds of files: text files and binary files. *Text files*, also called *ASCII files*, are the printable letters and numbers that make up a document that you see on your computer screen or output to a printer. These files contain no other codes, such as a word processor's formatting commands or the formulas of a spreadsheet cell, they just have alphanumeric text and perhaps carriage returns to mark the end of each line. Often, you can identify a text file because its file name has an extension such as .TXT or .ASC. The READ.ME files that come with many software programs are text files, and if you use the DOS TYPE command to display the contents of a file on your PC screen (for example, **C:\TYPE READ.ME**), you will be able to read the contents of the file as it scrolls by.

Binary files, on the other hand, consist of the most basic element of computer instructions: the combinations of 1s and 0s that computers understand as commands and data. Most of the files you have on your computer are binary files. They are the program files—with extensions such as .EXE and .COM—that run your applications. They are word processing files—with extensions such as .DOC, .SAM., and .WRI—containing both text and formatting information. They are spreadsheet files—such as .XLS and .WK1—with the data, formulas, and formatting included. They are graphics files—such as .BMP, .PCX, .GIF, and .EP—that specify exactly what an image will look like on your computer's screen. You can tell that a file is a binary file when you use the DOS TYPE command because it displays nonsense characters such as smiley faces, clubs, spades, and blocks—usually accompanied by a cacophony of beeps from the PC speaker.

It's important to differentiate between text and binary files because they can be received and sent differently. You can send and receive virtually any kind of file that can be stored on a computer, but *how* you transfer a file depends a great deal on what kind of file it is. The next two sections cover receiving text files and binary files, respectively. You'll learn how to send both types of files later in this chapter.

Receiving Text Files   Text files are probably the easiest type of file to copy from an on-line service to your computer. Ordinarily, your computer holds in memory some amount of the most recent information received while you are connected to a bulletin board system or an on-line service. Once the allocated memory is full, new information takes the place of information sent earlier. When you disconnect from the on-line source, the information is cleared out of the computer's memory. However, the communications software can make a copy of all the text that scrolls across your screen and save it in a file that you specify, allowing you to capture a file. This is done by opening what some software programs, such as Procomm Plus for Windows, call a capture file. With other programs, such as the Windows Terminal program, you select the Receive Text File menu item to use this capability. During a single on-line session, you can open and close one or several capture files to save only the information you want. Keep in mind, though, that when you capture on-screen text, you also capture all the prompts and menus that appear on screen.

Capturing files is easier than downloading them (see the section Downloading a File later in this chapter). Here's how it works. Say you log on to a bulletin board using the procedures discussed in Chapter 6. You are reading bulletin board messages and you come across one that gives the phone numbers for other bulletin boards in your area. You want to save this information, so you open a capture file, using the appropriate commands or menu items in your software. In Procomm Plus for Windows, for example, you would choose Capture File from the program's File menu. A dialog box opens asking you what file name you'd like to give to the information you are about to copy. Let's say you name the file BOARDS.TXT. When you click OK, Procomm Plus begins to save all the text that the bulletin board sends to your computer and all the information you send to the bulletin board, including system prompts and your replies. As the text rolls onto the screen, Procomm Plus copies it to the file called BOARDS.TXT. When you are done, close the capture file. To do this in Procomm Plus, you again choose Capture File from the File menu and the program closes the capture file.

Each communications package works somewhat differently, but the procedure—opening a capture file, reading the on-line information that you want to save, and then closing the file—is the same from program to program. To find out how your communications software captures files, consult your manual.

Receiving Binary Files   While receiving text files can be a straightforward matter of capturing text as it scrolls across the screen, receiving binary files is slightly more complicated. Copying binary files from an on-line source is truly downloading, and it

FILE CAPTURE

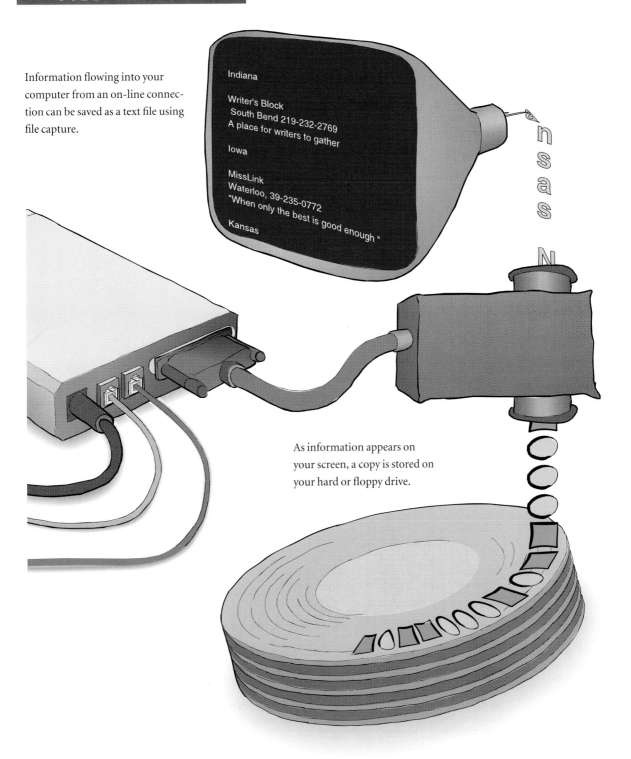

Information flowing into your computer from an on-line connection can be saved as a text file using file capture.

Indiana

Writer's Block
South Bend 219-232-2769
A place for writers to gather

Iowa

MissLink
Waterloo, 39-235-0772
"When only the best is good enough "

Kansas

As information appears on your screen, a copy is stored on your hard or floppy drive.

involves a few more steps than does capturing a file. In very simple terms, it works like this: First you identify the file you'd like to download and tell the service to download the file to your computer. Then the on-line service and your computer have a little *tête-à-tête* about how the two systems will talk to one another. When the two agree—with or without some intervention from you—the on-line service sends the file to your computer while you sit back and enjoy a hot cup of mocha java. When you download a file, you don't see the file's contents scroll across the screen as you do when you capture a text file. Instead, once you start to download a file, you'll notice that your hard-drive light is on, and you'll probably see a message on screen telling you how much of the file has been copied to your computer.

That, of course, is the overview. To actually download a file, you'll need to know a little bit about just what the on-line service and your computer are talking about when they put their heads together. Essentially, they are agreeing to the terms of the exchange: the *file transfer protocol* (sometimes also called the *communications protocol*), which is the topic of the next section.

FILE TRANSFER PROTOCOLS

The file transfer protocol simply outlines the way the remote on-line service and your computer talk to one another as a file is sent from the remote system to your computer. It specifies the flow of information from one system to another and outlines how the sending and receiving computers verify that the data arrived at its destination free from errors. This latter process is called error-checking.

To visualize this process, imagine that the file to be transferred is like a barrel of water that resides on the remote computer. Your computer has an empty barrel of the same size waiting to be filled with the water that's in the barrel on the remote computer. The file transfer protocol is the water carrier between the two systems. It determines the size of the bucket that will transport water between the two barrels, fills the bucket on one end, empties it into the waiting barrel on the other end, and checks to make sure nothing has spilled along the way.

N O T E   *Although you can easily capture ASCII text, you can download most ASCII files, too. You download ASCII files just as you do binary files. And when you download ASCII files, you get the pure text files without all the on-line service's screen prompts sprinkled into the text.*

Each protocol accomplishes essentially the same task: sending data accurately from one computer to another. But each does this according to somewhat different rules. Why are there so many sets of rules? A sports analogy might best explain it. Baseball is baseball whether it's Little League, Major League, or some level in between. But while the basic elements of the game are the same, the specific rules by which each league plays are different. The different rules determine not only the way the game is played, but also the character of the game. A baseball game with no called strikes, for example, takes longer to play than a game with an umpire calling every pitch. And both teams must play by the same rules for the game to be a success. The same is true for file transfer protocols—they determine the rules and the character of the exchange.

Which file transfer protocol you use depends in some measure on your situation. First and foremost, you must choose a file transfer protocol that is supported by both your communications software and the bulletin board system or on-line service you are using. For a file transfer to happen at all, both the sender and the receiver must use the same protocol. The protocol you choose depends on a number of other factors as well, including the size of the file you're transferring and the speed at which your PC is communicating with a remote source. File transfer protocols differ in how they divide data, how they check to ensure that data is error-free, how they correct for faulty data transmissions, and—perhaps most important to on-line users—how quickly they do all this work.

ERROR CHECKING AND FILE TRANSFER

The file transfer protocol checks to ensure the data has arrived at its destination intact. If not, the protocol asks the sending computer to resend the incomplete or damaged section.

Resend bucket:
3,347,373

There are more than a dozen file transfer protocols. I mentioned Zmodem in Chapter 5, but you'll also find Xmodem, Ymodem, CompuServe B+, Kermit, variations to most of these, and a handful of others. To get a better sense of which protocol you should choose for certain situations, let's take a look at a handful of the most popular ones.

Xmodem is one of the oldest and most widely used protocols. It sends data in small blocks of 128 bytes, checks that the data was sent accurately, and then goes on to send the next 128 bytes of data until the entire file is transferred. Because these data blocks are so small, Xmodem is rather slow, at least relative to more advanced file transfer protocols. This slowness isn't evident when you transfer files at modem speeds of 1,200 bps, which was considered fast when Xmodem was developed. Nowadays modem speeds of 9,600 bps and faster are the norm, and Xmodem is showing its age.

Xmodem begat Ymodem, which sends data in blocks of 1 kilobyte. These larger blocks make Ymodem more efficient and significantly faster than Xmodem because it can send in one "trip" the same amount of data Xmodem sends in eight. The only downside of this increased block size is that if an error occurs somewhere within the 1-kilobyte block, Ymodem has to send the entire 1-kilobyte block again, whereas Xmodem needs to send only the smaller 128-byte block. As a result, Xmodem could actually be a more efficient file transfer protocol if you live in an area where the phone system is victim to line noise that introduces errors into file transfers, thus requiring blocks of data to be resent. One other benefit of Ymodem, though, is that it lets you send more than one file in a single transfer, whereas Xmodem requires that you transfer one file at a time.

You may also run into a variant of Xmodem call Xmodem-1K, which, like Ymodem, transfers data in 1-kilobyte blocks. But Xmodem-1K lacks a valuable feature of Ymodem: the ability to transfer multiple files in one transfer. That's why you might sometimes see Ymodem referred to as Ymodem/Batch.

Zmodem is the most recent link in this evolutionary chain of protocols. Rather than sending data in blocks, Zmodem sends it in a continuous stream and places error-checking codes throughout the file. Once the entire file arrives at its destination, the data

THE XMODEM FAMILY AT WORK

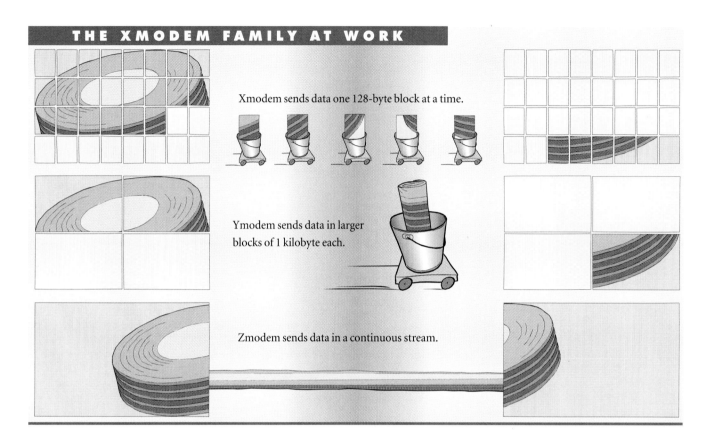

Xmodem sends data one 128-byte block at a time.

Ymodem sends data in larger blocks of 1 kilobyte each.

Zmodem sends data in a continuous stream.

is checked for accuracy. If there is an error, the appropriate section of the file is retransmitted. As you might guess, Zmodem is typically faster than either Xmodem or Ymodem. And it has one other significant benefit: If your file transfer is interrupted in the middle of the downloading operation, Zmodem remembers where it left off, checks the file at the receiving end, and restarts the download from there when you try again.

Xmodem and its progeny are designed to transfer files that use an 8-bit character format, so they generally are not suited for transfers between mainframe computers, which use a 7-bit format. To get around this limitation, a programmer at Columbia University came up with a new protocol that translates 8-bit characters into 7-bit characters. This new protocol was named Kermit, after the famed Muppet frog. It's worthwhile to know about the Kermit protocol, because you'll run into it in most communications programs and in many bulletin board systems and on-line services. Then again, you're not likely to actually *use* Kermit in the downloading situations you'll usually encounter.

It's a rather slow file transfer protocol, and most mainframe to PC connections will support some other more efficient protocol.

In fact, the protocol you'll probably use may be one you'll never really see. Many on-line services, especially those that require their own communications software to access the service (such as Prodigy and America Online), use proprietary file transfer protocols. On these services, there is no protocol for you to choose or set up. Instead, you select the command to download a file, and the service and your computer do the rest. Similarly, CompuServe has a proprietary protocol known as CompuServe B+. CompuServe B+ is a very fast protocol used specifically for transferring files to and from this on-line service, and many communications software programs support the protocol, as do CompuServe-specific communications program such as the CompuServe Information Manager (CIM) and WinCIM, both for the PC, and Navigator for the Macintosh.

DOWNLOADING A FILE

All this discussion about file transfer protocols may leave you thinking that downloading is a hassle and something you'd best stay clear of. In fact, it's a very simple process. To give you a better sense of how downloading works, I'll step through a typical downloading scenario.

Essentially, there are 5 steps to downloading a file:

▶ *Dialing into the bulletin board*

▶ *Finding the file you'd like to download*

▶ *Selecting a file transfer protocol*

▶ *Beginning the download*

▶ *Logging off the bulletin board*

Of course, this list omits a few of the finer details, so here are the specifics for dialing a bulletin board service called Channel 1, which is known for offering thousands of downloadable files.

Start by using your communications software to make the connection (see Chapter 6). Enter the Channel 1 phone number into your dialing directory, and set the usual communications parameters—parity: none; data bits: 8; stop bits: 1; duplex: full. When you dial into Channel 1, follow the on-screen prompts to register for the service, just as you would for any other bulletin board system. Once you're registered, the prompts help you find your way around the service. By typing **J FREE** at the prompt, for example, you'll see all the files that can be downloaded at no cost.

The next step is to find the file or files you'd like to download. There are two ways to do this. If you know the specific file or type of program you're looking for, say, the shareware game Wolfenstein or arcade games, you can use Channel 1's menu command Z to search for the program. If you're not looking for something particular, but just want to see what's available on the system, use the F command at the main menu to see a directory of files. (Incidentally, these and other commands are clearly defined on screen, making it easy to find your way around.) As you browse through the directory, you'll see a list of file names, an indication of the size of each file, and a brief description of each program. If something strikes your fancy, use the F command to mark—or *flag*—the file or files you'd like to download.

Once you've identified a file you'd like to have, choose D to download the file to your computer. Channel 1 tells you approximately how long it will take to complete the download, the size of the file or files to be downloaded, and the protocol it expects to use, based on information you gave the system when you registered. At this point, you can change the protocol, but make sure you have selected the same protocol in your communications software as you have on the service.

When you've decided on the protocol, press Enter. The system prompts you to tell your communications software to start downloading, and you choose the appropriate command in your software—probably Receive File, Download, or some obvious variation—to begin. Channel 1 and your computer exchange protocol information, and the download is underway. The bulletin board system announces when the download is complete, and you've done it—your first download. Now you can browse the bulletin board for more files, download other files, read messages, or log off. You needn't log on and off a service for each download.

Managing Downloaded Files   Downloading is a great way to bring lots and lots of data and software programs to your computer. But it's also very easy to create some real hard-disk messes—unless you follow a few simple rules of thumb.

Tip 1:   **MAKE A DIRECTORY OR A FOLDER ON YOUR HARD DISK** where you'll store all your downloaded files. I have a directory on my PC called \ZIP where I keep all the compressed files that I download.

Tip 2:   **WHEN UNCOMPRESSING A FILE, ALWAYS DO SO TO A NEW DIRECTORY OR FOLDER.** This way you won't find yourself trying to sort out a mess of files, some of which belong to the newly decompressed program and others that belong with other programs. This also makes it very easy to scan the program for viruses before you run it and to delete the program if you decide you don't want to keep it. And because you keep the compressed version in another directory or folder, you still have a copy of the program should you change your mind.

Tip 3:   **ALWAYS, ALWAYS, ALWAYS SCAN NEWLY DOWNLOADED AND UNCOMPRESSED FILES FOR VIRUSES BEFORE YOU RUN THEM.** If your scan turns up a virus, immediately delete the program and notify the bulletin board from which you downloaded it that the program is infected.

THE FIVE SIMPLE STEPS OF DOWNLOADING

1 Dial into a bulletin board or on-line service.

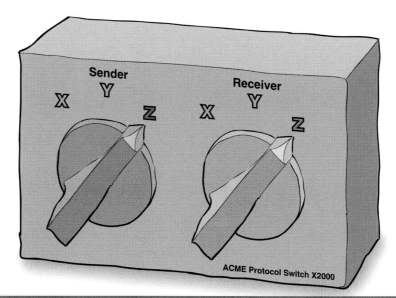

3 Select the file transfer protocol from those supported by both your software and the bulletin board or on-line service.

2 Find the file you want to download.

4 Begin the download.

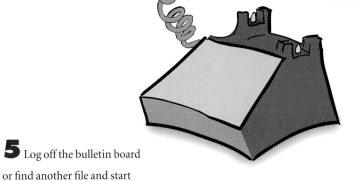

5 Log off the bulletin board or find another file and start downloading again.

SENDING TEXT AND BINARY FILES

Of course, file transfer is a two-way street. You can upload as well as download or capture files. It isn't oversimplifying the matter to say that uploading is the inverse of downloading. Rather than the file being sent from the on-line service to your computer, the file is sent from your computer to the on-line service. That's not to say that you follow the downloading steps in reverse, however; there are a few variations. Again, you log on to the service, but instead of looking for files, you determine where you are able to upload files on an on-line service. At the appropriate prompt, tell the service that you want to upload a file, agree on matters of protocol, and then instruct your computer to send the file.

You can send text files somewhat more simply by using the ASCII uploading feature available in most communications software. Most often, you use an ASCII upload to pour a text file that you've saved on your computer into a bulletin board or electronic mail message just as if you typed the entire file from the keyboard. To do so, prepare your written message before you get on line and save it to a file. Now, go on line and prepare a bulletin board or electronic mail message as you typically would, but when it's time to write the body of the message, choose the communications software's command to send or upload a text file. The program prompts you to enter the name of the file, for example, MESSAGE.TXT. Enter the file name, press Enter, and watch the text in the file scroll into the body of the message just as if you were typing the text into the message.

COMPRESSING AND DECOMPRESSING FILES

To make file transfers go more quickly, bulletin board systems and on-line services *compress* files to make them smaller. Compressing a file is a bit like freeze-drying coffee. By removing the water, you reduce a cup of coffee to a teaspoon of powder. Likewise, compressing a file lets you represent the file with a smaller amount of data. You may have heard the term zipped to refer to a compressed file. That's because most bulletin

COMPRESSING FILES

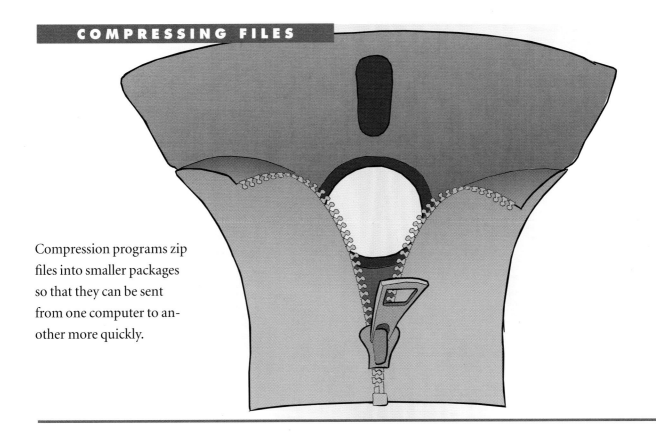

Compression programs zip files into smaller packages so that they can be sent from one computer to another more quickly.

boards and on-line services use a program called PKZIP to compress files that are PC compatible. Macintosh files are most frequently compressed using a program called StuffIt. You'll find copies of these programs on virtually all bulletin boards, and it's a very good idea to make one of these compression programs your very first download, because you'll need it to decompress the file once it reaches your computer. Just as a teaspoon of powdered coffee becomes a full cup of steaming brew only after you add hot water, a compressed file becomes usable again only after it's decompressed (or, as you'll sometimes hear, *unzipped*). You'll also want to compress files before you upload them to make the transfer go more quickly.

NOTE   *Incidentally, compressing files is a great way to save hard-disk space. You can compress infrequently used files, decompressing them only when you need to use them.*

ON-LINE SERVICES

America Online

CompuServe

Delphi

GEnie

Prodigy Information Service

ZiffNet Information Service

Apple Link

Thoughout this book you've come across references to on-line services and bulletin board systems. But just what are they and what's the difference between them? To some degree, defining them differently may seem like technical nitpicking. On-line services are large, commercial information services. They run on a network of large mini- and mainframe computer systems accessible through a telecommunications network that enables you to call a local phone number and log on to services around the world. Bulletin board systems are small, often not-for-profit message and downloading forums. They run on a personal computer or a small network of personal computers accessible through only one phone number.

On-line services and bulletin board systems differ, too, in the amount and kind of content they offer. On-line services are storehouses of information, shopping services, software catalogs, news services, electronic mail, financial data, and the like. Bulletin boards usually provide an extensive downloadable file collection, a public message system, and perhaps some on-line, interactive games and news.

Perhaps the best way to clarify the difference is to think of the two as communities. Indeed, the world of on-line services and bulletin board systems truly is a community, a place as real as any you'd find in a Michelin guide. On-line services are like large towns or significant cities, while bulletin boards are like smaller, often isolated enclaves. Just like each place on a map, every major on-line service and bulletin board system has a unique flavor. In this chapter, you'll begin a guided tour of on-line services. Then, in Chapter 9, you'll take a closer look at some very interesting bulletin board systems.

Incidentally, entire books have been written about each of these major on-line services. In the space I have here, I'll try to acquaint you with the character of each service, highlight some of its special features, and give you a sense of how you will find your way around the service when you log on. And remember, when you join any of these services, you will receive a new member guide to help you discover all the service's secrets.

AMERICA ONLINE

Imagine rolling down a long desert highway and coming to an oasis. The sheriff meets you at the city limits, welcomes you like a long-lost neighbor, and gives you a personal tour of the city. As you drive down Main Street—past coffee shops, the post office, the library, the newspaper office, a gaming parlor—the locals stop their conversations and come out of the storefronts, smiling and waving. Welcome to America Online, the country's friendliest on-line service.

AOL, as the locals call it, is a gossipy community of some 350,000 where people are quick to throw in their two cents. But if they come for the conversation, they stay for the range of information available at one of the best prices around. You'd expect news, sports, weather, stock quotes, and travel services—and AOL has them all. Dig a little deeper and you'll find a substantial reference library, including Compton's Encyclopedia, the Library of Congress database, the *Time* magazine archives, and the Hoover's Handbook database of public and private company profiles.

The first things most visitors notice when they arrive on AOL is the abundance of on-line chatter. If you could actually *hear* the exchanges, your ears would ring with the cacaphony of dozens and dozens of conversations. Members talk about the day's headlines and the latest sports scores. They help one another to better use computers. They share their enthusiasm for fiction, science fiction, and nonfiction. They flirt, argue, and laugh with one another. In short, if there's something you want to talk about, there's someplace on AOL to talk about it. Many of these conversations take place in a chat area called The Meeting Place. But there are special scheduled conferences, too. AOL's Center Stage is an on-line auditorium that hosts talk shows with entertainers, writers, musicians, politicians, and other public figures. You'll also discover weekly gab sessions

AMERICA ONLINE

America Online greets you with this welcome screen each time you log on, highlighting the newest aspects of the service.

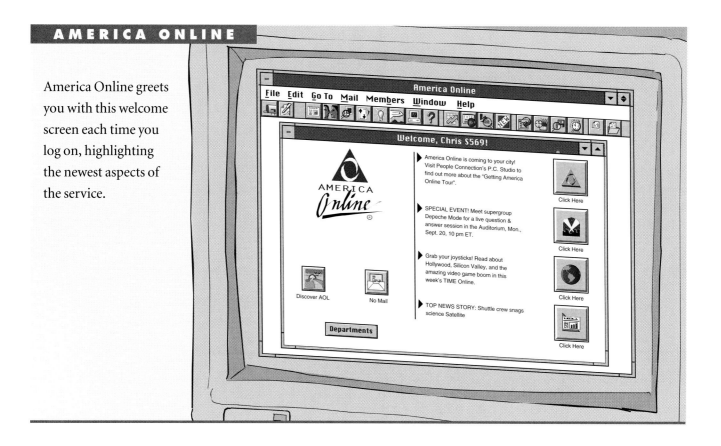

hosted by a variety of groups. To find out what's happening when, just check AOL's Directory of Services where you will find an up-to-date calendar of events.

But AOL isn't all idle chatter. Among the service's unique offerings is the Microsoft Small Business Center, a cooperative effort among Microsoft, AOL, and some 20 companies and business associations, including the U.S. Small Business Administration, the U.S. Chamber of Commerce, and the National Federation of Independent Business. The center provides a collection of articles on business concerns—such as marketing, government regulations, and financing—and hosts on-line seminars offered by such groups as the American Management Association. You'll find software programs and spreadsheet templates that address the unique problems of small-sized businesses. And you'll find *real people*. Each Wednesday evening, volunteers from SCORE, the Service Corps of Retired Executives, get on-line to provide individual counseling about your specific business conerns.

America Online's graphical software is a literal floor map of the AOL grounds. Click on the newspaper icon and move quickly to the service's news and information area. The airplane icon takes you to travel services, the game icon to entertainment options, and so forth. Each time you log on to AOL, you get a complete rundown on the newest happenings, so it's easy to keep abreast of service changes. From the main greeting screen, you can also take a tour of AOL, a good idea for new users. The tour highlights some of the most popular features and provides a directory of the complete service. Even after you've been an AOL member for a while, you may want to stop by the tour on occasion just to find out what's new.

Once you know your way around, you can use AOL's keywords to zip immediately from one section to another without having to wade through menus at all. And if you get lost at any time, you can summon help by clicking on the question mark icon. This will take you directly to the Member's Online Support area where you'll find America Online customer support representatives standing by, ready and willing to help you find what you are looking for.

See the handy keyword boxes in Chapters 11 and 12 to learn more about what's on AOL.

AMERICA ONLINE

ESTABLISHED: 1985

POPULATION: 350,000

SITES OF INTEREST: Microsoft Small Business Center; Electronic University Network (where you can earn a college degree on line).

LOCAL COLOR: Check out any "room" where members go to chat with one another.

COST: $9.95 per month for 5 hours of use. Additional time costs $3.50 per hour.

TOURIST INFO:
America Online, Inc.
8619 Westwood Center Dr.
Vienna, VA 22183
800-827-6364; 703-448-8700

CompuServe

If America Online is a down-home town full of heartland folks, CompuServe is a metropolis teeming with business, activity, ideas, noise, and excitement. But don't expect to be greeted at the border by eager guides. To the newcomer, CompuServe feels a bit like getting into Grand Central Station at 3 a.m.: You're not quite sure in which direction to head and it's hard to find people to ask. Once you get your bearings, though, you'll find that CompuServe is loaded with news, business data, financial reports, travel services, and lots of information about computing. Any hardware or software company that even dreams of being successful has a forum on CompuServe to talk with customers.

Like any big city, CompuServe is jam-packed with local hangouts for scores of professional groups. CompuServe calls these gathering spots *forums* and hosts hundreds of them to meet a range of special interests. They are *the* place for like-minded people to find one another and swap war stories, tip one another to job opportunities, and keep up-to-date on happenings in their fields. There's the Entrepreneur's Small Business forum, an information exchange sponsored by *Entrepreneur Magazine*, and the Working from Home forum, a lively network of home office workers. There are special forums for computer consultants, journalists, pilots, lawyers, and public relations pros, among others. On CompuServe, you can talk to your peers around the world, exchanging ideas and uncovering new avenues for business.

Along with these coffee-shop-like forums you'll find one-stop shopping for everything from computers and software to business suits and flowers in the CompuServe Electronic Mall. Many of the on-line stores are familiar catalog companies: Columbia House, Direct Micro, Hammacher Schlemmer, Lands' End, and the Metropolitan Museum of Art. Others are national chains, such as Barnes & Noble, JC Penney, Brooks Brothers, Sears, and Walden Computer Books. And there are some unique shopping services, including the AutoQuot-R automobile pricing service. Through these outlets, you can buy products and have them shipped just about anywhere in the world.

CompuServe is an invaluable resource for businesses with questions; it is like a New York Public Library of research resources for people who have neither the time to get to the library nor the resources to hire a research staff. With more than 1,700 databases and 1.4 million members, CompuServe is bound to have the answer to your question.

With so much information, it's easy to get lost. If you've just arrived, there are a few keys to finding your way about and a couple of sites that should be on your itinerary. CompuServe can be navigated by digging down through menus and then climbing back up to try another option, but by using *GO words* you can quickly zip from service to service. At the CompuServe prompt, if you type GO followed by the name of a CompuServe area—for example, NEW—you bypass the menu system and go directly to the area called NEW. In this case, GO NEW takes you to a listing of the latest features and events on CompuServe. Incidentally, you'll most often see CompuServe's GO commands printed in uppercase letters, but you can enter them in upper- or lowercase when you are on the service.

The handy keyword boxes in Chapters 11 and 12 provide some go word examples.

For a basic monthly fee, CompuServe offers unlimited access to a number of service areas. Additionally, CompuServe offers a cursory tour that highlights the contents of its major service areas and provides a free Practice Forum where you can learn how to use the service efficiently without the pressure of paying by the minute.

If you are serious about tapping into CompuServe's vast resources, I recommend getting on line and downloading a copy of WinCIM, the CompuServe front-end communications program for Windows. Simply put, a *front-end program* serves as a go-between for you and an on-line service. The front-end program interprets menu selections or graphical icons into the commands necessary to navigate to an area of an on-line service and perform the requested tasks. WinCIM is a graphical interface that turns CompuServe's sometimes complex navigational commands into icon buttons that you can click to jet from one part of the service to another. WinCIM also automates many

tedious chores, such as sending and receiving mail and collecting messages from various

forums. You'll find WinCIM by entering **GO WINCIM** at the CompuServe prompt.

CompuServe offers a Macintosh version of its front-end program called MacCIM.

You can find it by entering **GO MACCIM** at the CompuServe prompt.

COMPUSERVE

ESTABLISHED: 1979

POPULATION: 1.4 million

SITES OF INTEREST: Working from Home forum (GO WORK); Entrepreneur's Small Business forum (GO

USEN); Dun's Electronic Business Directory of 8 million professionals and businesses (GO DYP); Business Data-

base Plus (GO BUSDB), which is a library of 450 business and trade publications.

LOCAL COLOR: Check out any personal interest forum where you'll quickly find out what's on each partici-

pant's mind.

COST: The standard pricing plan is $8.95 per month and covers access to some content selections. All other

services carry connect charges of $8.00 for 2,400 bps access or $16.00 for 9,600 bps.

TOURIST INFO:
CompuServe Information Service
5000 Arlington Centre Blvd.
P.O. Box 20212
Columbus, OH 43220
800-848-8990; 614-457-8600

DELPHI

Relative to the rapidly growing on-line services with which it competes, Delphi looks a bit like a ghost town these days. But behind those tumbling weeds and squeaking saloon doors, there is still an active community of on-line chatters and game players who take advantage of Delphi's relatively inexpensive rates. And the recent purchase of Delphi by media mogul Rupert Murdoch may turn this ghost town into a boom town once again.

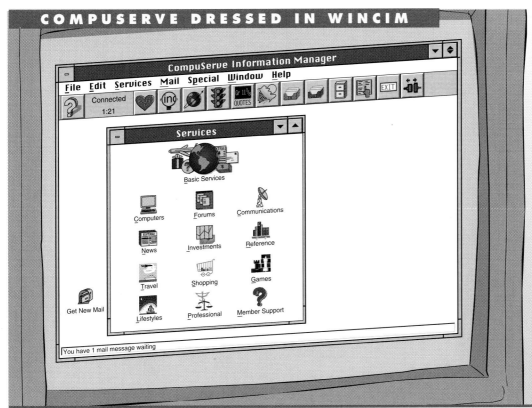

COMPUSERVE DRESSED IN WINCIM

Access CompuServe using any communications software, and you'll see the service in character mode. Use CompuServe's WinCIM communications program, and you'll have a graphical view into the service that looks like this.

Delphi is just this side of a plain and simple bulletin board, but it does offer a host of services for the information junkies. Delphi offers access to business and financial news and database services; timely news, sports and weather information; an AIDS information network; the *Dictionary of Cultural Literacy* and *Grolier's Encyclopedia*; a health database; the *NYNEX Yellow Pages*; and even an on-line directory of gourmet recipes. If you can't find what you're looking for, Delphi has a librarian who will research just about any topic you request—for a fee, of course.

But most notably, Delphi is a low-cost gathering place for a variety of special interest groups. You'll find groups in support of different computers, among them the older or less popular systems, such as the Amiga, Apple II, Atari, Tandy, and Commodore. There are hobbyist groups for UFO watchers, musicians, photographers, writers, theologians, and environmentalists. Plus, there are nightly open conferences, where members can join in free-for-all discussions of just about anything.

DELPHI MAIN MENU

Delphi lists its content options in the main menu, but it requires that you type the name of the area you want to visit, rather than providing a numbered choice, as do other services.

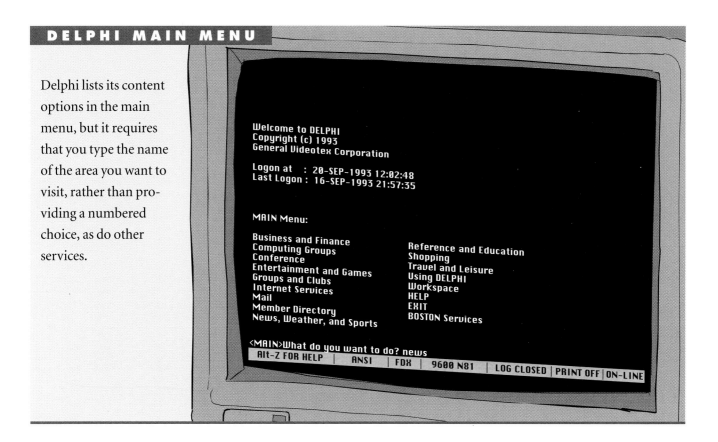

```
Welcome to DELPHI
Copyright (c) 1993
General Videotex Corporation

Logon at   : 20-SEP-1993 12:02:48
Last Logon : 16-SEP-1993 21:57:35


MAIN Menu:

Business and Finance
Computing Groups          Reference and Education
Conference                Shopping
Entertainment and Games   Travel and Leisure
Groups and Clubs          Using DELPHI
Internet Services         Workspace
Mail                      HELP
Member Directory          EXIT
News, Weather, and Sports BOSTON Services

<MAIN>What do you want to do? news
 Alt-Z FOR HELP  |  ANSI  |  FDX  |  9600 N81  |  LOG CLOSED | PRINT OFF | ON-LINE
```

Delphi is a text-based service: Words roll by on the screen and you make your way through the service by typing your menu selections at the prompt. Delphi doesn't offer the equivalent of CompuServe's GO words or America Online's keywords. Instead, you dive down into layers of menus to see more options revealed below. When you hit bottom, you use the EXIT command at each level to make your way back to the top, where you catch your breath, and start digging again. Fortunately, all of your choices are clearly described on screen, and Delphi quickly sends new members a "command card" that clearly explains the services and how to move from place to place. To get the best sense of the service and some of its special commands, take Delphi's Guided Tour, found under the Using Delphi menu choice.

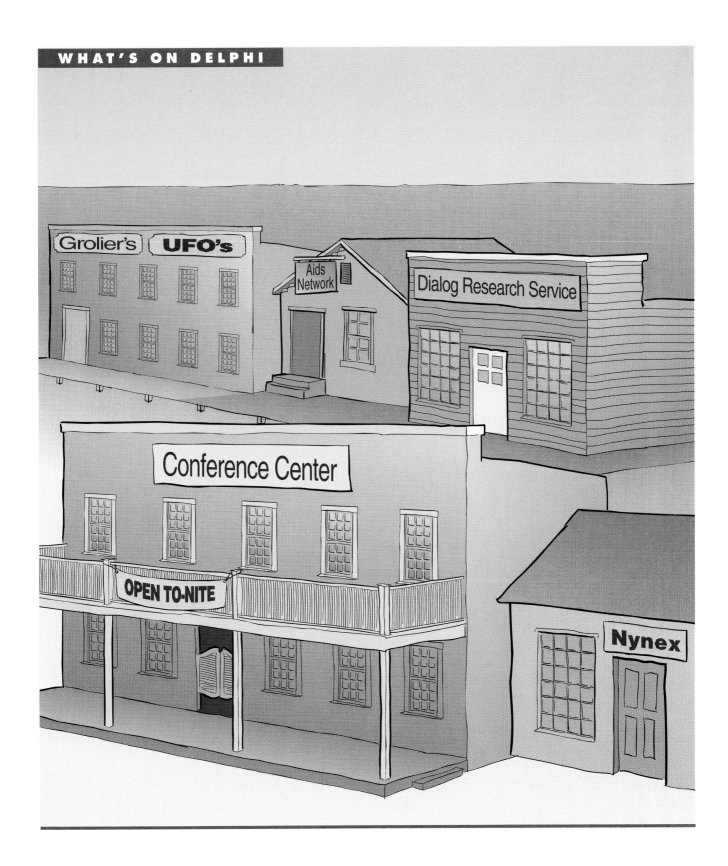

DELPHI

ESTABLISHED: 1981

POPULATION: 120,000

SITES OF INTEREST: Delphi's groups and clubs appeal to people with a wide range of special interests, from hobbies to politics to business. MensNet chronicles the men's movement; the Environment Special Interest Group discusses global ecology; WIDNET provides information on disability policy from the World Institute on Disability. The Delphi Librarian is a special service that tracks down information when you just can't find what you're looking for.

LOCAL COLOR: Check out Delphi's Conference to meet some of the interesting characters who gather to talk each evening.

COST: Delphi offers a 10/4 Plan, which, for $10.00 per month, lets members use the service for 4 hours each month and pay 6.6 cents for each minute thereafter. The 20/20 Advantage Plan gives members 20 hours each month for $20.00, plus a one-time enrollment fee of $19.00. After 20 hours, Delphi charges 3 cents for each additional minute.

TOURIST INFO:
Dephi/General Videotext Corp.
1030 Massachusetts Ave.
Cambridge, MA 02138
800-694-4005; 617-491-3393

GENIE

More than a city, GEnie is a fantasyland. It is the game player's dream come true. Sure, it has the news and research features you find on other on-line services. There's news from Reuters, Newsbytes, Dow Jones, the Sports Network—even a clipping service. Business people get a resource directory, career services, company profiles, credit profiles, and a patent database. The GEnie Mall offers wares from a host of mail order and direct marketing companies. You'll find on-line technical support for a wide range of computer products from companies like Borland, IBM, Tandy, Apple, GeoWorks, Hayes, Microsoft, and WordPerfect. These companies also participate in on-line discussions.

But GEnie's real appeal is games, and lots of them. There are multiplayer games that you play with other GEnie members. Classic adventure games that take you to the

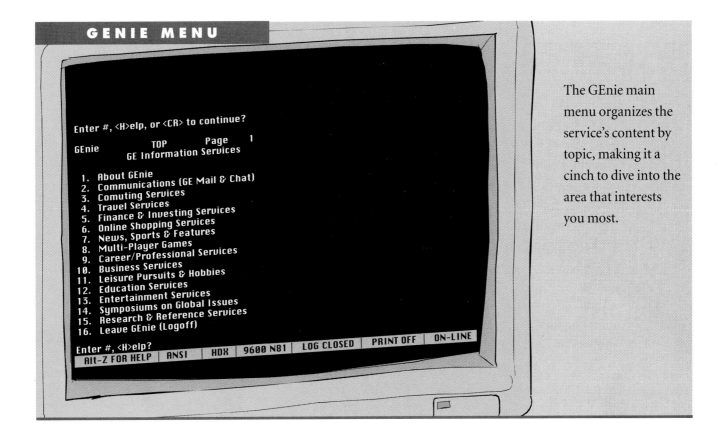

GENIE MENU

```
Enter #, <H>elp, or <CR> to continue?

GEnie          TOP        Page     1
          GE Information Services

   1.  About GEnie
   2.  Communications (GE Mail & Chat)
   3.  Comuting Services
   4.  Travel Services
   5.  Finance & Investing Services
   6.  Online Shopping Services
   7.  News, Sports & Features
   8.  Multi-Player Games
   9.  Career/Professional Services
  10.  Business Services
  11.  Leisure Pursuits & Hobbies
  12.  Education Services
  13.  Entertainment Services
  14.  Symposiums on Global Issues
  15.  Research & Reference Services
  16.  Leave GEnie (Logoff)

Enter #, <H>elp?
 Alt-Z FOR HELP │ ANSI │ HDX │ 9600 N81 │ LOG CLOSED │ PRINT OFF │ ON-LINE
```

The GEnie main menu organizes the service's content by topic, making it a cinch to dive into the area that interests you most.

depths of dreary castles. War games. Space games. Strategy games. Games you can lose yourself in for a very long time. Spend some time delving into Castle Quest (but watch out for the werewolf) or doing battle with on-line friends in a game of Air Warrior. Plus GEnie offers a ton of games that you can download and play off-line. And when you get tired of playing games, you can talk about them, exchanging tips and hints or just getting to know your on-line opponents.

GEnie hosts a variety of *roundtable discussions* on just about any topic imaginable: aviation, pets, photography, electronics, scuba diving, writing, food and wine, motor-cycling, books, law, medicine, real estate, the military, show business, science fiction, comedy, religion, disabilities, Japan, Canada, travel—just to name a few. Like other on-line services, GEnie also schedules regular on-line meetings of special interest groups so you know exactly when to log on for a chat.

WHAT'S ON GENIE

Like Delphi and CompuServe, GEnie is a text-based service, using menus to usher you around. You don't have to dig through menus to find what you're looking for, however. GEnie arranges information in "pages" and you can go directly to that information by using either the page number or keyword. Of course, you have to know the page number or keyword to take advantage of this method of zipping from one area to another. GEnie sends you a directory of the services when you enroll that lists both the page numbers and keywords for most information. You'll also see the keyword and page number at the top of each screen as you navigate around the service. (See the handy keyword boxes in Chapters 11 and 12.)

But the toughest challenge is cracking into GEnie in the first place. When you dial into GEnie the first time and subsequent times, you are greeted with a screen that's blank except for an obscure U# prompt. The first time you call the service, type **SIGNUP**, and from there you can follow essentially English instructions for joining the service. On subsequent calls, you type your user ID followed by a comma and your password, then press the Enter key before you'll see even a hint of the English language.

GENIE

ESTABLISHED: 1985

POPULATION: 350,000

SITES OF INTEREST: Have I mentioned games? Use the keyword MPGAMES to enter a brave new world of on-line gaming and adventure.

LOCAL COLOR: Check out the evening's discussion roundtables for a very interesting slice of life. You'll meet people of all ages and interests and have a good time jumping in and out of conversations.

COST: GEnie charges $8.95 per month, which covers your first 4 hours of connect time each month. After that, you pay just $3.00 per hour, with a $9.50 surcharge for use of the service between 8 a.m. and 6 p.m. local time. If you connect at 9,600 bps, it will cost you an extra $6.00 hour.

TOURIST INFO:
GE Information Services
401 N. Washington St.
Rockville, MD 20850
800-638-9636; 301-340-4000

PRODIGY INFORMATION SERVICE

If America Online is a heartland town and CompuServe a metropolis, Prodigy is a sprawling suburban highway, lined with malls, take-out restaurants, gaudy billboards, and the occasional professional building. It is, more than any other, the on-line service for the mainstream American family.

Prodigy offers world, national, business, sports, and entertainment news; shopping services; chatty columns on business travel, international business, working from home, taxes, and technology; and mountains of bulletin board messages about whatever Prodigy members happen to have on their minds. The format of the service is modeled after print publications. Information is presented in colorful graphic screens, complete with advertisements for everything from cars and clothing to software and sunglasses.

Though many users complain about these ads, the ads serve to keep the cost of Prodigy low. And that makes one of Prodigy's strengths—its financial services—a significant bargain for most business people. Prodigy provides regularly updated business and stock-market news, stock quotes, company profiles, an investor's glossary, an electronic version of *Kiplinger's Personal Finance* magazine, and a handful of columns from top-rated money advisors. Most of these services are available for a monthly flat rate of $14.95, with additional hourly or membership fees levied for special services, such as the ZiffNet for Prodigy computer special interest and software downloading service.

Prodigy also provides some convenient personal financial services at reasonable prices. The service features an investment advisor called Strategic Investor, which provides mutual fund and stock reports for a fraction of the price charged on other services. There's even a handy electronic bill-paying service, called BillPay USA, and an on-line discount stockbroker, called the PC Financial Network.

Prodigy's other great strength is its community of some 2 million members. The member profile is a slice of life, representing the largest percentage of women online, for example, as well as an age range that spans younger children through retirees. With 750

Prodigy's highlights give you the hour's top news headlines, along with instant access to the most popular areas of the service.

public message topics, it's a safe bet that you'll find someone on Prodigy with whom you can share ideas and exchange information about running a small business, for example.

Each time you log on to Prodigy, you are greeted by a bright highlights screen that keeps you abreast of what's new across the service. This screen acts as a menu that takes you immediately to the hot news of the day. If you have some other destination in mind, choose Prodigy's *JUMP command* to move directly to the information you want. The JUMP command is found on the service menu. You can type in the destination or choose your destination from a readily available index. Because most of Prodigy's services are available for one monthly fee, you can be leisurely about exploring the service. Just keep an eye on the bottom-right corner of the screen, where you can always tell whether you are in an extra-cost service area or not.

The keyword boxes in Chapters 11 and 12 will direct you to interesting places.

PRODIGY INFORMATION SERVICE

ESTABLISHED: 1990

POPULATION: 2 million

SITES OF INTEREST: Strategic Investor investment advisor (JUMP SI), Money Highlights for all the latest business news (JUMP MONEY HIGH); Quote Check for 15-minute delayed stock quotes (JUMP QUOTE CHECK).

LOCAL COLOR: Check out the Prodigy Exchange bulletin board, where members are all too happy to share their views of the service.

COST: The Value Plan provides unlimited use of most service features and up to 2 hours of premium services for $14.95 per month. A second plan, priced at $8.79 per month, provides 2 hours of use for any Prodigy services. Additional time is billed at $4.80 with discounts for extended use.

TOURIST INFO:
Prodigy Information Service
445 Hamilton Ave.
White Plains, NY 10601
800-PRODIGY

ZIFFNET INFORMATION SERVICE

ZiffNet Information Service is an enclave, a city if you will, in the heart of the CompuServe metropolis. A private service dedicated to personal-computer-related information, ZiffNet uses the CompuServe network to reach its audience of dedicated computer professionals and enthusiasts. ZiffNet was born as a companion on-line service to computer publications including *PC Magazine, PC/Computing, PC WEEK, Computer Shopper, MacWEEK,* and *MacUser.* In a little more than two years, it has become the gathering place for computer industry insiders.

The Executives Online forum, a discussion center focused on new computer products and breaking industry news, has entertained the likes of Phillippe Kahn, the dynamic and outspoken CEO of Borland International; Ted Waite, the outrageous head of mail order giant Gateway 2000; most of Microsoft's top management; and the IBM OS/2 product marketing team. This forum is a rare opportunity for the *consumers* of computer products to talk to, question, debate, and deride the *developers* of computer products.

Baseball Manager

Golf Tournament

NOVA stories

Strategic Investor

PC Financial Network

National Geographic Adventures

PC Flowers

U.S. Postal Service

Consumer Report·

Take a look at the new FUN & GAMES

Computer Club ZiffNet Selections

American & United Airlines

Need to check a few stoc· Try QUOTE CHEC·

Visit the Prodigy Traveler KNOW WHERE TO GO!

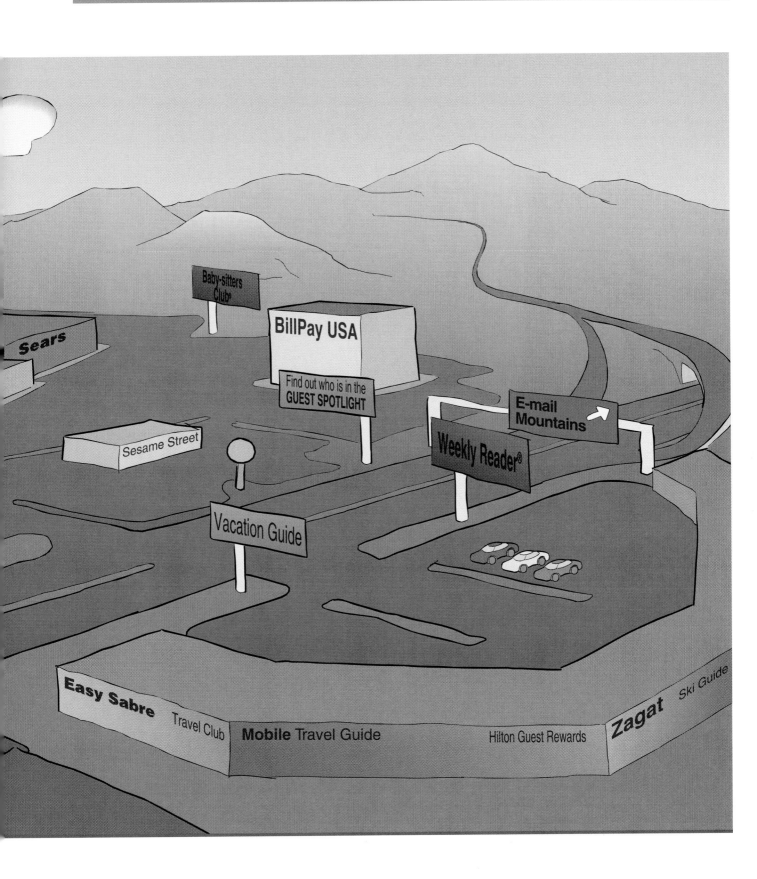

Each day, ZiffNet
highlights the hottest
events happening
around the service.

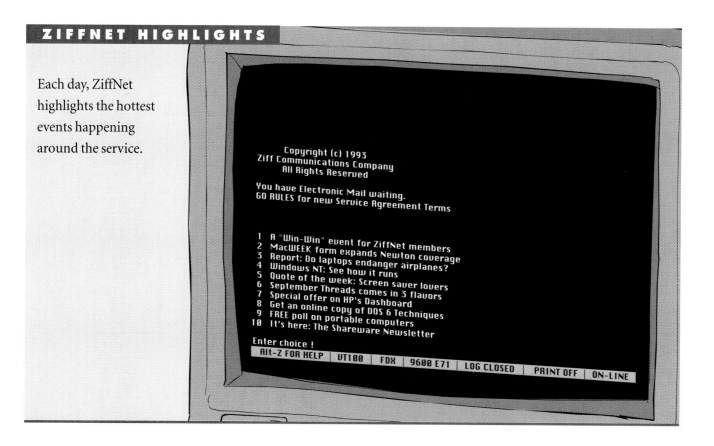

Copyright (c) 1993
Ziff Communications Company
All Rights Reserved

You have Electronic Mail waiting.
GO RULES for new Service Agreement Terms

1 A "Win-Win" event for ZiffNet members
2 MacWEEK form expands Newton coverage
3 Report: Do laptops endanger airplanes?
4 Windows NT: See how it runs
5 Quote of the week: Screen saver lovers
6 September Threads comes in 3 flavors
7 Special offer on HP's Dashboard
8 Get an online copy of DOS 6 Techniques
9 FREE poll on portable computers
10 It's here: The Shareware Newsletter

Enter choice !
Alt-Z FOR HELP | UT100 | FDX | 9600 E71 | LOG CLOSED | PRINT OFF | ON-LINE

In addition to this lively forum, ZiffNet provides a carefully culled library of top-rated shareware programs. These programs, which you can copy from the service to your computer, run the gamut from word processors, spreadsheets, and databases to computer housekeeping utilities, specialized data, and unique specialty applications. Each program in this library has been evaluated and determined to be of a quality that rivals its more expensive commercial counterparts. ZiffNet employs a band of sysops (system operators) who are happy to recommend programs to outfit a home office.

You'll also find the popular *PC Magazine* utilities on the ZiffNet service. These utilities, discussed in each issue of *PC Magazine*, can be downloaded for free by typing **GO PC-MAGUTIL** at the ZiffNet prompt. (See the handy keyword boxes in Chapters 11 and 12.)

But ZiffNet isn't just a safe haven for computer junkies. It's a lifesaver for anyone who has a computer problem and needs to get it fixed—now. The service includes a database called Support on Site (SOS) that enables you to search the documentation—

often there are also unpublished technical notes of hundreds of hardware and software products. Frequently, a search of the SOS database pinpoints the problem and renders a solution in the time it takes to get through to most technical support departments.

Because ZiffNet is built on top of the CompuServe system, you get around ZiffNet just as you get around CompuServe. ZiffNet does have its own custom version of WinCIM that replaces the general service icons with ZiffNet-specific icons. And you'll want to be sure to get a copy of the service map that comes in the ZiffNet new member kit. This map differentiates services that charge connect time fees from those that don't.

Z I F F N E T   I N F O R M A T I O N   S E R V I C E

ESTABLISHED: 1991

POPULATION: 160,000

SITES OF INTEREST: PBS software library (GO PBSAPPS) and its collection of thousands of shareware and freeware programs; Executives Online forum (GO EXEC) to meet the movers and shakers of the computer industry; PC Magazine forum (GO PCM) to talk with the editors of *PC Magazine*.

LOCAL COLOR: Check out the After Hours forum (GO AFTERHOURS) to find out what computer junkies talk about when they aren't talking about computers.

COST: $2.50 per month, including free access to select services. Connect time charges of $12.80 per hour for 2,400 bps access or $22.80 for 9,600 bps access apply to all other areas. Less expensive rates are available to CompuServe members.

TOURIST INFO:
ZiffNet Information Service
25 First St.
Cambridge, MA 02141
800-848-8990

AppleLink

AppleLink is somewhat different from other commercial on-line services in that it is a product-support resource specifically for Macintosh and Macintosh-related products. Unlike other on-line services that are filled with games and chats and encyclopedias and the like, AppleLink provides 24-hour access to Apple and third-party product

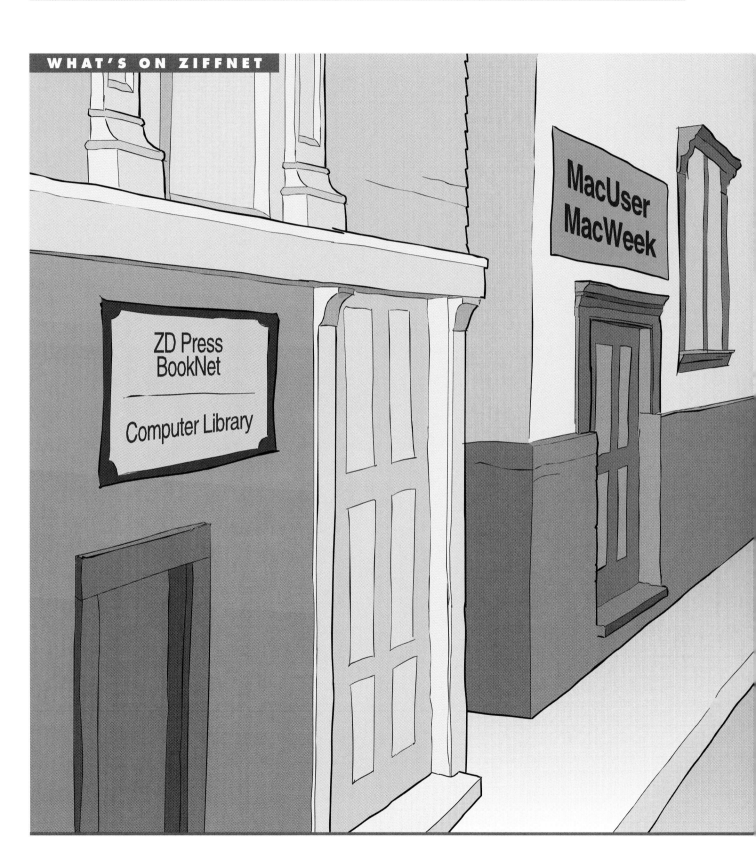

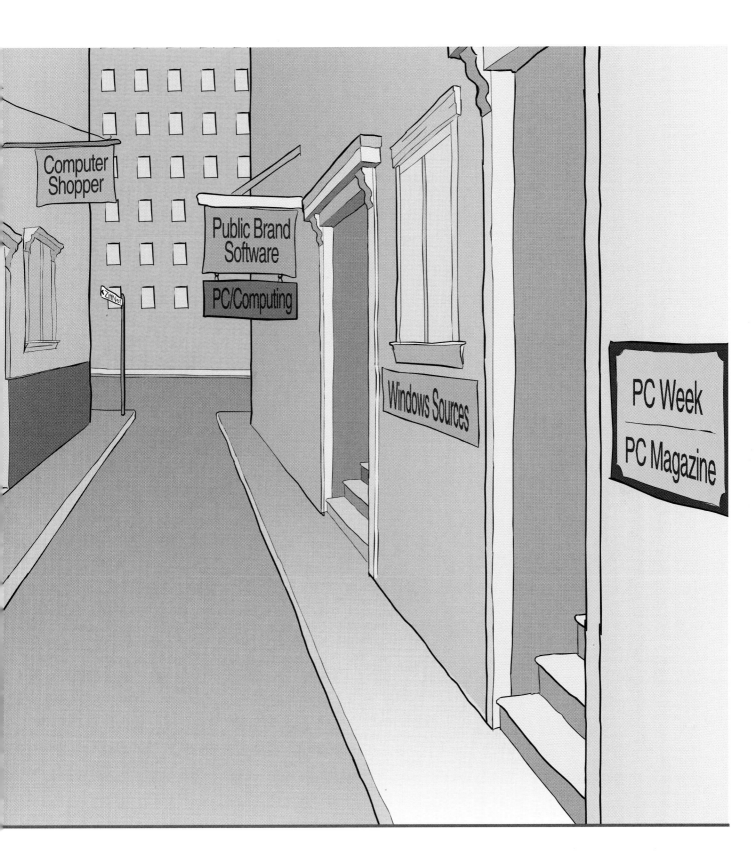

technical support. AppleLink maintains a library of technical information on line. If you can't find the answer to your question there, you can send a message to a tech-support mailbox or post the question on the public bulletin board. Typically, you'll have a response in less than 48 hours.

This prompt and efficient service comes at a price. AppleLink is considerably more expensive than other on-line services. You'll pay a one-time start-up fee of $70.00, and then a monthly minimum fee of $12.00. The regular hourly connect fee is $12.00, with additional fees charged for the amount of information you access while on line, measured in units the service calls *kilocharacters.* One kilocharacter is 1,000 text characters and costs 4.5 cents during off-peak hours. If you want to access the service at 9,600 bps, you'll pay an extra $37.00 for the privilege. At those prices, AppleLink appeals more to Macintosh professionals than to the general public.

For more information, contact AppleLink at Apple Computer, P.O. Box 10600, Herndon, VA 22070, 408-974-3309.

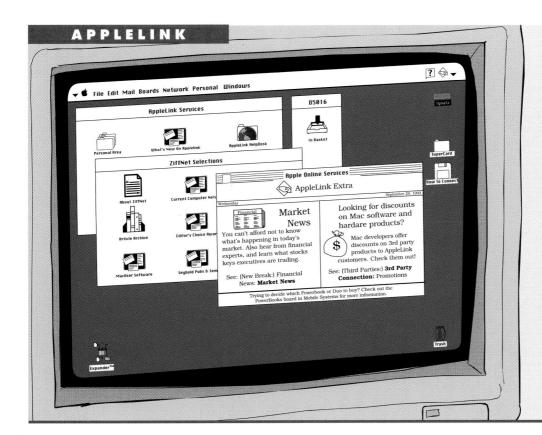

AppleLink highlights broadcast what's new on the service. The AppleLink Services menu neatly organizes on-line content into Mac-like folders.

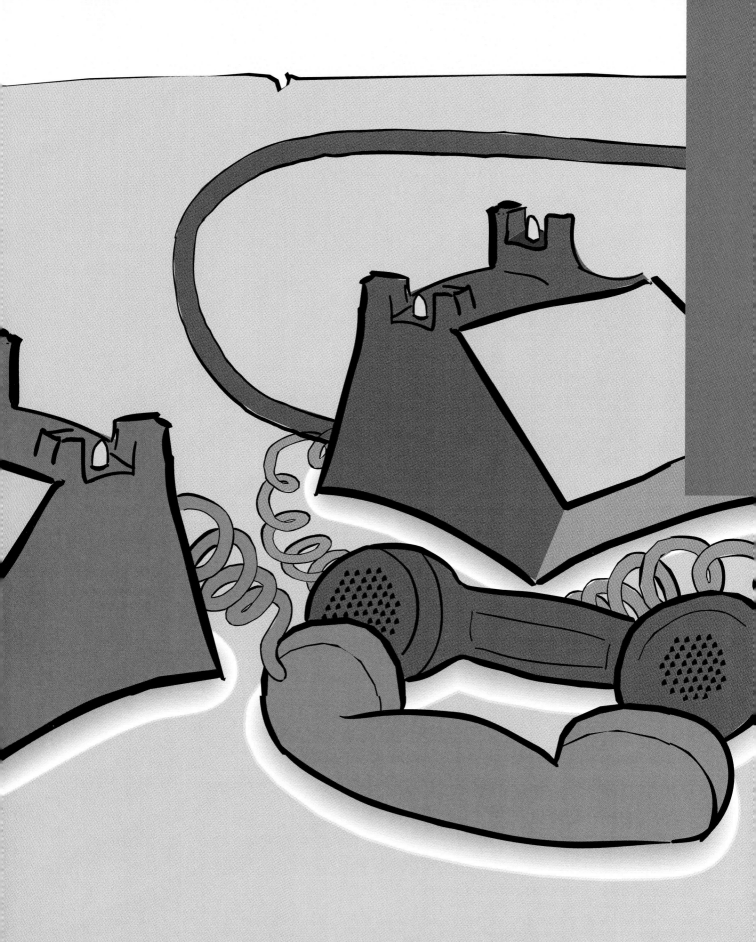

BULLETIN BOARD SYSTEMS

9

You'll never be lonely as long as you have a modem. With some 50,000 bulletin board systems throughout the United States, there's always somebody to talk to. Bulletin board users talk about the news of the day, swap stories about most anything, argue politics, and confide in one another. They share their secret recipes, celebrate each other's victories, and lend advice on any problem at hand. Bulletin board systems are virtual town picnics and electronic swap meets. Bulletin boards range in tone from cordial conversations among the newly acquainted to raunchy, off-color remarks you would never hear in polite company. It all depends on where you call. But no matter, you're in for a wild ride where opinions fly faster than supersonic jets and people gather for no other reason than the pleasure of your company.

WHAT ARE BULLETIN BOARD SYSTEMS?

Bulletin board systems are small on-line services that are as ubiquitous as neighborhood taverns. They are friendly electronic meeting places where people feel comfortable with one another. You'll have little trouble finding a bulletin board system in your local calling area. Indeed, anyone with a computer, modem, and shareware bulletin board software can launch an on-line service—and many individuals have. More likely, though, you'll first hear about the bulletin boards sponsored by computer users groups or community service organizations. Government agencies use bulletin boards to share public information. Software junkies set up bulletin boards to feed their shareware habits, collecting and distributing literally thousands of software programs, sound bites, graphics, and data files on line. You'll also discover that many hardware and software companies provide bulletin boards where you can ask questions about their products. These bulletin boards provide technical support if you have a problem using a product, and they often include files that you can download and use with the product. Some of these files fix bugs in software programs or are drivers that enable products—such as a graphics package and a printer—to work together. Others are templates and macros to enhance the product.

More interesting than the sheer number of bulletin boards is the huge breadth of fascinating topics discussed in these electronic communities. What are your interests? There's a bulletin board out there somewhere to serve them. As you'd probably expect, there are bulletin boards dedicated to specific hardware systems, software applications, operating systems, programming languages, and the like. But these are just the tip of the iceberg. There are bulletin boards about books, videos, camping, exotic birds, ham radio, treasure-hunting, weather, sports, lifestyles, wildlife conservation, AIDS, reptiles, job-hunting, legal issues, genealogy, convention planning, Mayan culture, the environment, sailing, conservative politics, liberal politics, earthquake data, disability rights, botany, games (take a deep breath now), and even bulletin boards about other bulletin boards.

The advantage to bulletin board systems is that they are usually inexpensive, relative to the major commercial on-line services such as CompuServe, America Online, Prodigy, and the like (see Chapter 8). Moreover, you are likely to find a handful of bulletin board systems in your area that offer many of the same software programs and interesting conversations as you might find on commercial services. The downside is that some local bulletin board systems may not be as reliable because they are not handled by full-time, professional operators, but instead by part-time hobbyists. Moreover, there are limits to the amount of time you can spend on some systems and the amount of information you can download. And some bulletin board systems may propagate illegal copies of software and may not ensure that programs on their services are virus-free.

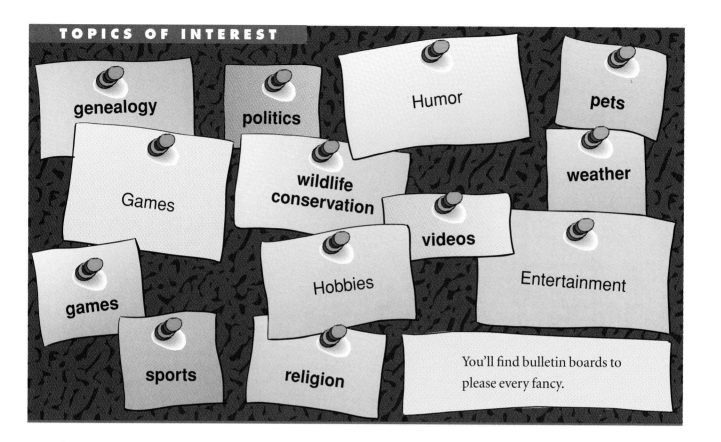

TOPICS OF INTEREST

genealogy
politics
Humor
pets
Games
wildlife conservation
weather
videos
games
Hobbies
Entertainment
sports
religion
You'll find bulletin boards to please every fancy.

HOW TO FIND A BULLETIN BOARD

With so many bulletin boards of such a wide variety, how do you find a bulletin board that suits your fancy? The best answer is to apply circular logic: Find a bulletin board by finding a bulletin board. Discovering bulletin boards is a lot like exploring caves. As you do your on-line spelunking, you'll trip upon the names and numbers of other bulletin boards. And by exploring those boards, you'll find out about other boards, and so on, and so on. Perhaps your local computer users group or a nearby computer store has a bulletin board. Try that board and look for messages referring to other boards or post a message to other users. Many users are familiar with other bulletin boards and are happy to share their opinions of boards and provide you with phone numbers.

Another way to find a bulletin board is through *Boardwatch Magazine,* which attempts to keep track of the sprawling bulletin board boom. The magazine (the annual subscription fee is $36.00, which you can send to 7586 West Jewell Ave., Suite 200, Lakewood, CO 80232) regularly publishes a list of bulletin boards throughout the United States and Canada. In addition to its databases of bulletin board systems, *Boardwatch* also runs a bulletin board (303-973-4222) that carries news from *USA Today* and the Newsbytes computer industry news service.

SUBSCRIBING TO A BULLETIN BOARD SYSTEM

Once you find the bulletin board system you want to subscribe to, logging in is easy. Chapter 6 takes you step by step through the process of calling a bulletin board and logging in. That's exactly the procedure you will use to subscribe to any bulletin board system. You won't need special software and there's no need to preregister, as is the case with some commercial on-line services. Instead, you do all the signing up on line. Typically, you are asked for your name, address, and phone number. The bulletin board asks you to select a password and asks you to type it again to confirm it. Then you are introduced to the features of the service, the pricing plan if there is one, the benefits of joining, and you're asked to subscribe.

Many bulletin board systems use the same software to run their services. As a result, once you've logged in to one bulletin board system, you'll know how to log in to most any other bulletin board. And once you've mastered one bulletin board system, you're well on you way to understanding how they all work. Most let you browse through the board for some amount of time, but ask you to subscribe if you'd like to spend more time on the board, leave messages, or download files. But just as you might get a sample copy of a magazine, you can sample the bulletin board system before subscribing. Most boards let you explore the service for 30 to 60 minutes before subscribing. Of course, you may not have access to all the service's capabilities during this trial period.

Bulletin board subscriptions work just as those to magazines do, but rather than paying for a set number of issues, bulletin board users subscribe to a number of minutes, months, or years they can use the service. Typically, these fees run from a few dollars a month to annual or even lifetime subscriptions costing about one hundred dollars. These subscription fees entitle you to some amount of time to use the service, or perhaps some specific amount of data you can download from the service, or both. Some bulletin boards let you earn time on the service by giving you credit for files you upload or messages you post. Other services let you use the service without subscribing, but limit the amount of time you can be on the service and the amount of information you can access. Then again, some bulletin boards are absolutely free and have no use restrictions. But even bulletin boards that are free track callers and may limit the amount of time you can spend on the board during a single call and perhaps even the total time you can use the board during a day or a week.

These various ways of operating bulletin boards can be confusing, so be certain to read the system's log on announcements and review its subscription terms carefully before signing up. Incidentally, most major bulletin boards accept MasterCard and VISA for payment of subscription fees.

To get a sense of how all these subscription plans might work, look at Exec-PC, the self-proclaimed "largest BBS in the world." Exec-PC has three levels of users:

▶ *A demo caller can use the service for 60 minutes each day, but can only download files from a limited free library, read messages in the MS-DOS area, and scan the on-line want ads. Demo callers are not able to post messages, but can leave comments with the system operator, or* sysop, *when they log off.*

▶ *A paid caller can subscribe for 3 months for $25.00 or for a year for $75.00 and have full access to everything on the service, including thousands of downloadable files. Paid callers can use the service for up to 600 minutes and download up to 7 megabytes of data each week.*

▶ *Free uploader status lets callers earn time on the service by uploading files and posting messages. Exec-PC does limit the number of callers who can register as free uploaders, so don't be surprised if this subscription option is not available to you.*

Before you subscribe to any service, it's a good idea to read the regulations you will be expected to live by. The rules give you a sense of the flavor of the service and may help you decide whether or not to subscribe.

For details, see the section Minding the House Rules, later in this chapter.

Local Access Companies   Whether a bulletin board is free or not, you still must calculate the cost of the phone call in the overall price of the service. If the bulletin board system is a local number, you pay nothing in telephone charges. If you dial long distance to reach the service, you pay the phone charges for the time you spend connected to the bulletin board, just as you pay the phone charges for the amount of time you talk to your mother-in-law over voice lines.

But local access companies make it much less expensive for you to call long-distance bulletin boards. With local access companies, you call a local phone number, and in turn the local access company makes the long-distance connection with the bulletin board. You pay nothing for the local phone call, but instead pay a fee—usually much lower than the phone company would charge—to the local access company.

One of the larger local access companies is G-A Technologies, which provides the Global Access service. Using Global Access you can call virtually any bulletin board service for just $4.00 per hour (about 7 cents per minute) during the off-peak hours of 6:00 p.m. to 7:00 a.m. local time and all day on weekends and holidays. Global Access charges a one-time set-up fee of $20.00 and a $10.00 monthly membership fee that includes 2 hours of off-peak use. Global Access has a special deal with nine bulletin board systems, including the popular Exec-PC and Rusty -n- Edie's, so you are charged only $2.95 for off-peak use and $9.95 during peak hours. Global Access is available from 22,000 local phone exchanges, covering most metropolitan areas. You can find out more about the service by calling their voice line at 800-377-3282 (outside the United States, the number is 704-334-3282) or by dialing into their information-packed bulletin board at 704-334-9030.

PC Pursuit is a less expensive but significantly smaller local access company. For a $30.00 registration fee and a $30.00 per month charge, you can use a local access number to reach bulletin board systems in 44 major metropolitan areas. That $30.00 monthly fee gives you 30 hours of access time, a rate equal to 1.6 cents per minute, during the off-peak hours of 6:00 p.m. to 7:00 a.m., weekends, and holidays. PC Pursuit provides the service to about 400 local exchanges. For more information, call 800-736-1130 or 703-689-6400.

FINDING YOUR WAY AROUND A BULLETIN BOARD

If you can imagine a bulletin board system as a large house, you'll begin to get a clear picture of how information is arranged on a bulletin board. In fact, many bulletin boards will use terms such as *rooms* or *doors* to describe the areas where information of different kinds is stored. For example, all bulletin boards have a public entrance way, a foyer, so to speak. This is where callers are greeted, asked to log on, and told of new features on the service or of new service policies. Moving around the house, you'll likely find one or more rooms where members can go to talk with one another, either in a conference with a number of members, or one on one in a private chat. The bulletin board may even provide separate rooms depending on the topic under consideration. You'll almost always find a library, too, where members go to browse through descriptions of downloadable files. There may be a reading room where electronic messages, news, and magazine articles are available to read on line. And most services have the on-line analog to a mail room, where members send uploaded files. The files stay in this room until the sysop can sort them, scan them for viruses, and deliver them to the appropriate spot in the library.

As you try different bulletin boards, you'll find that the various "houses" are constructed differently. Once you get the feel for one, however, exploring the next and the one after that becomes much easier. Moreover, the menus in the bulletin board serve as a floor plan to help you find your way around.

MINDING THE HOUSE RULES

All bulletin board systems have some set of house rules, even if the rules are that there are no rules. These rules set the tone for the bulletin board, and you agree to abide by them when you subscribe to the service. They detail what language is unacceptable in bulletin board messages, what kinds of files may not be uploaded to the system, and may even set a minimum age requirement for members.

Generally, bulletin boards prohibit profanity or overtly obscene content in public messages. You are not permitted to defame the character of other board users, a rule that may include infractions ranging from name-calling to accusations of wrongdoing. Some boards, usually those that cater to adult conversation and downloadable material, require users to pledge that they are 18 years of age or older.

The rules of the service are set and monitored by the board's sysops. The sysops act as referees, monitoring messages for fair play and bouncing anyone who fails to abide by the rules. Once you join a service, if you fail to comply to the service rules, your subscription may be terminated without refund.

CONFERENCES AND CHATS

Conferences and chats are among the most popular features of bulletin board systems (and many commercial on-line services, too). A conference is a real-time conversation among a group of people who happen to be on line together at the same time. (*Real time* means that information or data is exchanged immediately, rather than being stored for later retrieval. In real-time messaging, two or more on-line service users see one another's messages as they are being typed.) A conference usually occurs in a specific area of a service and often centers on a particular topic. A chat is a real-time conversation between two or more people, but it is usually less formal than a scheduled conference.

Conferences and chats work in essentially the same way. You enter the conference or chat area and type a message. When you press Enter, the message appears to other

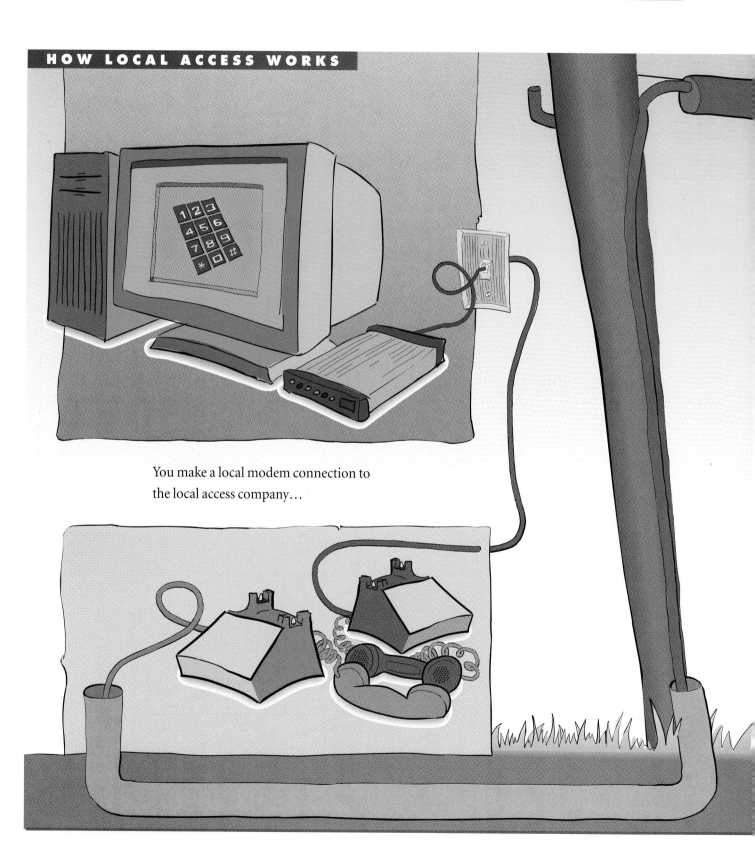

HOW LOCAL ACCESS WORKS

You make a local modem connection to
the local access company…

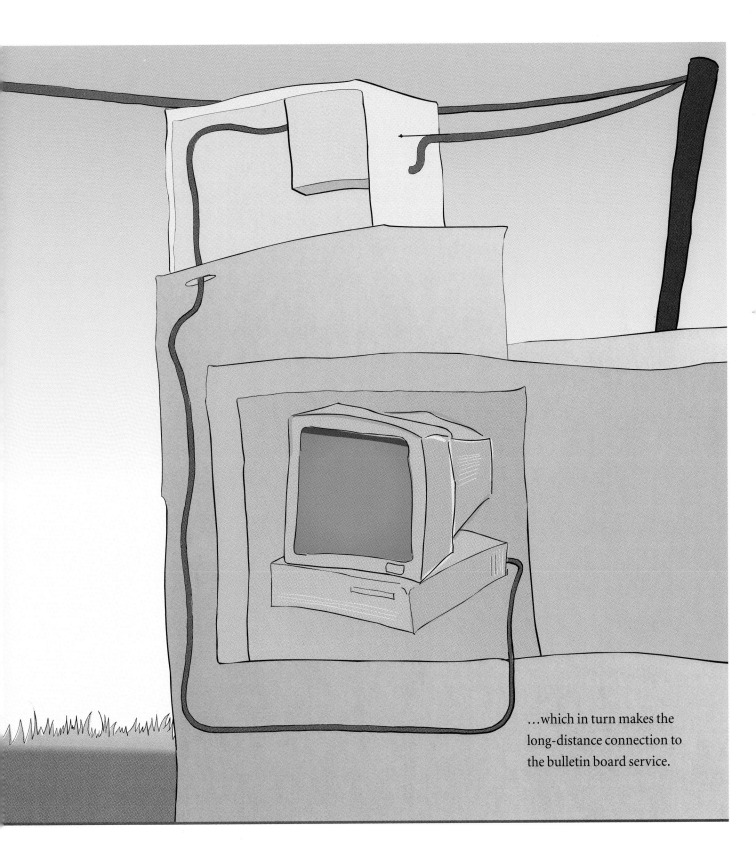

...which in turn makes the long-distance connection to the bulletin board service.

A BULLETIN BOARD IS LIKE A HOUSE WITH MANY ROOMS

**Private Chat
(Members only)**

Public Announcem

Conference Room

**Public
Entrance**

A bulletin board's menu provides the
floor plan to the service.

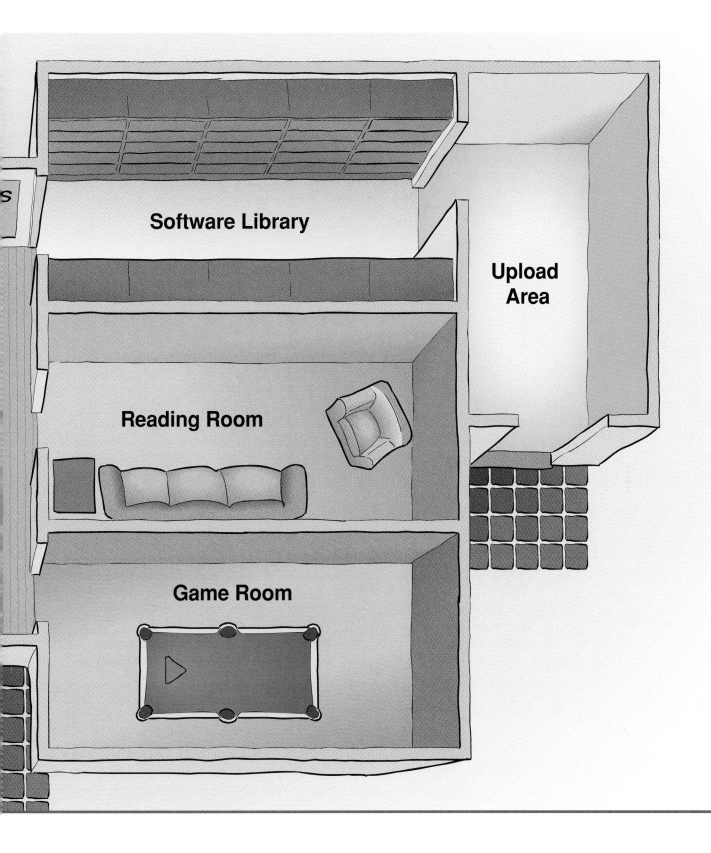

people who are in that area. The message appears next to your name, so that other people know who is saying what. See the illustration A Sample Chat Session.

Bulletin board systems and on-line services have a command, usually called something like "who," that gives you a list of other users on the service. In this way, you find out who, if anyone, is on line with you before you strike up a conversation. Bulletin boards and commercial on-line services also list scheduled conferences, either around a topic or a guest appearance. For example, there might be a writer's group that gets together on Thursday night at 9:00 or a Star Trek fan club meeting Saturday afternoon at 3:00. If you can't find a conference schedule on line, go to the conference area and ask what's available that might suit your interests.

Although conference and chat are terms that are generally used to describe real-time conversations, you're likely to see these called by other names, including CB Simulator (CompuServe), forums (CompuServe, America Online), round tables (GEnie), SIGs (Delphi), party lines, and COs (short for COnferencing).

BULLETIN BOARDS AROUND THE U.S.A.

With tens of thousands of bulletin boards available across the United States, choosing "the best" bulletin board systems is an impossible endeavor. The boards listed here were chosen to represent some of the most popular systems and to reveal the variety of bulletin boards available. Most, if not all, bulletin board systems can be accessed from any type of computer—IBM compatible, Macintosh, Atari, Commodore, even UNIX workstations. Once you connect, however, you may find that while you can participate in discussions and play on-line games, the board does not have downloadable files that are compatible with your computer. And one more noteworthy item: Bulletin board operators attempt to keep their costs low and change user fees as infrequently as possible. Nevertheless, the fees mentioned in this chapter are subject to change. For current prices, check the subscription or pricing bulletins posted on bulletin boards that charge registration fees.

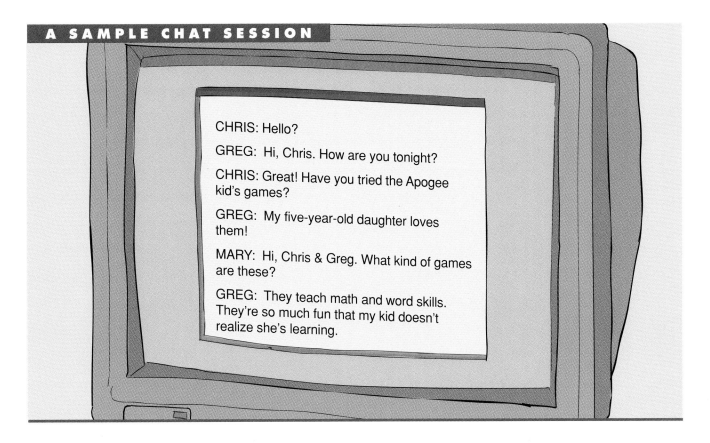

A SAMPLE CHAT SESSION

CHRIS: Hello?

GREG: Hi, Chris. How are you tonight?

CHRIS: Great! Have you tried the Apogee kid's games?

GREG: My five-year-old daughter loves them!

MARY: Hi, Chris & Greg. What kind of games are these?

GREG: They teach math and word skills. They're so much fun that my kid doesn't realize she's learning.

The Well (415-332-6106)   was launched in 1985 by the same people who published the *Whole Earth Catalog*. The Well is a meeting place for an eclectic and, some might say, eccentric group of hackers, writers, and counterculture cyberadventurers. The Well has over 200 conferences in a wide range of categories, including politics and social responsibility, education, computers, business, the media, health, cultures, arts, entertainment, and the Grateful Dead. This is the place to be if you want interesting talk, and you can connect from just about any type of computer.

Your first 5 hours on the Well have no connect time costs so you can explore the service at a leisurely pace and find the conferences that most interest you. Before signing up, you can sign on as a guest to read and download background information and sample some classic Well conversations.

Cost: The Well charges $15.00 per month, plus a $2.00 per hour connect time charge and an additional $1.00 per hour if you are connecting at 9,600 bps or faster.

Exec-PC (414-789-4210) claims to be the largest, busiest, most popular bulletin board system, and its claim is probably correct. On line since 1983, Exec-PC gets about 5,000 calls a day from 45 different countries. Indeed, when I first logged in to the service, I was caller number 6,840,560, and the service says it racks up another one million calls every 7 months. Exec-PC offers a job bank, real-time games, closing stock-market prices, an on-line magazine, and a discussion area that boasts more than a half-million messages. The giant software library includes files for PC, Macintosh, Amiga, and UNIX-based computers. The bulletin board is well organized with simple-to-follow menus, making it easy to explore this vast service.

Cost: You can join Exec-PC for $25.00 for 3 months or $75.00 per year, which lets you use the service for 600 minutes each week. You may be able to register as a free uploader and get credit for free use of the service. For each 10 minutes worth of file upload, you'll earn 40 minutes of on-line time.

Celebration Station (207-374-5161) is as friendly and enjoyable as a guitar-picking, toe-tapping evening of music. If the names Peter, Paul, and Mary have you whistling a tune about a magic dragon named Puff, then you'll want to log in to this bulletin board founded by Noel Stookey, the Paul of the famed folk trio. This board supports PCs and Macintosh, Amiga, and Atari computers.

You'll have no problem finding your way around the board's forums, file libraries, chat areas, and games. There's a nightly chat session at 9:00 p.m. You can try the service for 30 minutes a day for 60 days, with access to some files and forums, but you'll have to join the service to take part in the nightly bull sessions.

Cost: When you become a "by-gum certified user," you get your first hour on the service free. Additional time is 50 cents per hour with a 10-hour minimum purchase. You get a 10 percent discount by buying time in blocks of $25.00 or more.

Rusty -n- Edie's (216-726-0737) calls itself the "friendliest BBS in the world." It is a down-home bulletin board run by husband and wife team Russell and Edwina Hardenburgh. New users are invited to spend up to 60 minutes looking around the service, reading and posting messages, and playing its enjoyable, interactive games. Started as "an expensive hobby" free to all callers, the board became so popular that Rusty and Edie could continue only by soliciting "registered donors." Anyone can use the board for 60 minutes, but you can download only if you make a donation. Rusty -n- Edie's recently started a new Mac conference area with discussions of Mac-related topics and downloadable Macintosh shareware.

Cost: Donors of $69.00 or more have unlimited access to the service for one year and can download up to 10 megabytes per week. Donors of more than $40.00 but less than $69.00 have the same privileges for 6 months, and donors of $25.00 to $39.99 get access for 3 months. To demonstrate just how expensive a hobby running a bulletin board can be, Rusty and Edie say they've spent over $750,000 on the service since it launched in 1987.

Livewire BBS (609-235-5297) is appropriately named. Before you have a chance to log in you're confronted with the toughest decision of all: Which language do you want to use? Among your options: Jive Yakkity, Southern Twang, Australian DownSouth, Canadian Lingo Eh, Stooge Conversation, Star Trek Lingo, Body Building Arnold, Government Lingo, oh, and of course English. Choose Stooge and the prompts read differently from any bulletin board you've tried before. (See the illustration Stooge Conversation Prompts.)

The message sections are as odd a mix as are the system prompts, sprinkled in among Windows, PageMaker, programming, and job listings, were alien visitors, Howard Stern, UFO, and the Bible. And that's just the tip of this very weird iceberg. In addition to the message sections, Livewire provides a host of real-time interactive

STOOGE CONVERSATION PROMPTS

Listen Moe...I tink you should see all the pretty colors...Wanna?

Your first name Mug??

Now the last, birdbrain?

Passwoid Doc??

The log-in prompts of the Livewire BBS.

games, including Battleship, backgammon, chess, checkers, and Othello. You can play against other callers or against the computer.

You get up to 10 calls before you're nudged about registering with the service. As a free caller, you have limited access to service areas for 20 minutes per day and you have no downloading privileges.

Cost: You can register at a variety of levels, ranging from Entry Level at $50.00 per year or $20.00 for 3 months to Super Member, which costs $150.00 per year or $50.00 for 3 months. Each level gives you greater access privilege and more time on line.

Wizard's Gate (614-224-1635) is an interesting board that plays to the science-fiction crowd. Among its bulletins you'll find a list of all the original Star Trek Episodes, including a rating of their merits, a text file of Star Trek drawings, and even a Star Trek parody. The very best thing about this board is that it is absolutely free. In fact, they won't take your money even if you try to give it to them. You get 90 minutes for your first call and you can call up to nine times a day. There are tons of files for downloading and a variety of on-line games to play.

Cost: Free!

National Genealogy Society (703-528-2612) is dedicated to genealogical information. It doesn't offer games. It doesn't offer a software library of every shareware program ever created. There are no gimmicks or twists. But if you're a genealogy buff, you'll want to call this board. You can post messages for others, search a database for other genealogy bulletin boards in your local area, and find out about national meetings. The files available for downloading are all about genealogy, including family histories and software utilities for both the PC and Macintosh. You'll get 30 minutes to use the board each time you call, and there are no registration fees.

FIFTY NIFTY BULLETIN BOARDS

Legal Ease
Spokane, Washington
509-326-3238
Legal-acess database
for lawyers and the
public alike

Banished CPU
Portland, Oregon
503-232-6566
Supporting freedom
of speech,
controversy welcome

Private Idaho
Boise, Idaho
208-338-9227
Large section of odd,
controversial, and off-the-
wall Macintosh software

WestNet
Helena, Montana
406-458-9379
33,000 files and
counting

Blazing Icicle
Minot , North Dakota
701-839-0181
Specializing in
communications
hardware and software

After Hours Nightclub
Gillette, Wyoming
307-686-7358
Largest game list in
northeast Wyoming

Voyager
McCook Lake,
South Dakota
605-232-4648
Focused on astronomy
and hobby electronics

Buy This BBS
Las Vegas, Nevada
702-871-7982
Tons of business and
PC newsletters

Mages Inn
Omaha, Nebraska
402-734-4748
Specializing in
interactive multiuser
games

Eye of the Storm
Layton, Utah
801-546-6300
Utah's largest
adult-oriented BBS

Rainbow Missions
Boulder, Colorado
303-938-9654
Focused on the Bible,
Christianity, and
missionary support

**New World
Information Service**
Wichita, Kansas
316-262-1829
Features discussions
on home-brew beer

PC Sports Connection
Anaheim, California
714-533-6728
An on-line sports bar

Ranch and Cattle
Phoenix, Arizona
602-943-1497
The "most bizarre"
BBS in the world

The Garbage Dump
Albuquerque,
New Mexico
505-294-5675
An adults-only
playground

Vox Compuli
Oklahoma City,
Oklahoma
405-749-9906
Putting citizens in
touch with public
officials

The SMOF-BBS
Austin, Texas
512-467-7317
World's first on-line
science-fiction
convention

**The Wall Street
Connection**
Honolulu, Hawaii
808-521-4356
Focused on investing
and financial planning

Northern Exposure
Fairbanks, Alaska
907-479-3292
A colorful, game-filled
BBS

These bulletin boards, one from
every state in the Union, celebrate
the diversity of interests represented in the on-line community.

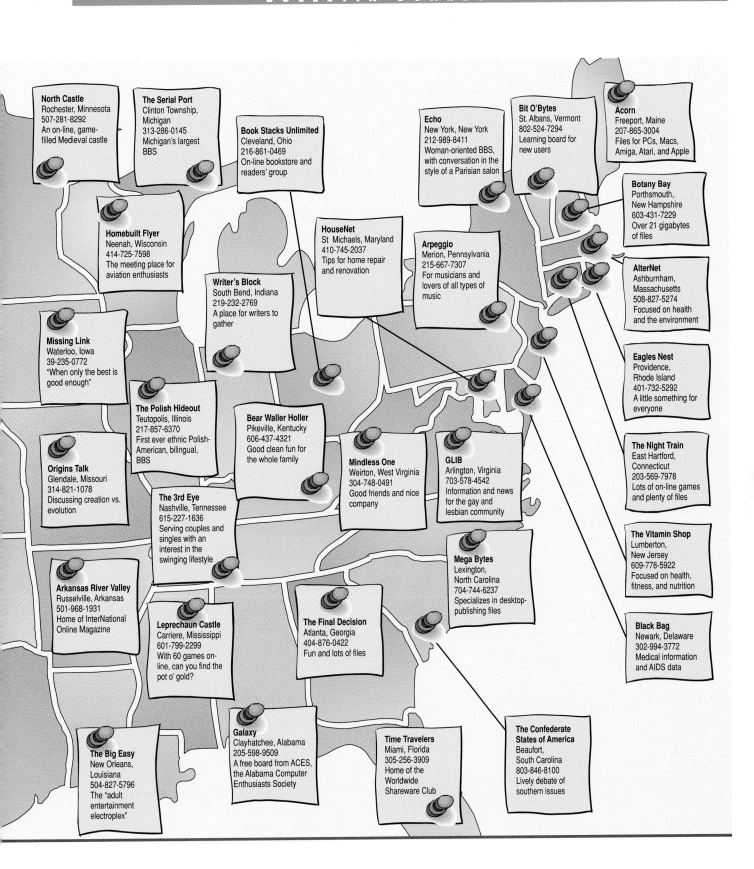

North Castle
Rochester, Minnesota
507-281-8292
An on-line, game-filled Medieval castle

The Serial Port
Clinton Township, Michigan
313-286-0145
Michigan's largest BBS

Book Stacks Unlimited
Cleveland, Ohio
216-861-0469
On-line bookstore and readers' group

Echo
New York, New York
212-989-8411
Woman-oriented BBS, with conversation in the style of a Parisian salon

Bit O'Bytes
St. Albans, Vermont
802-524-7294
Learning board for new users

Acorn
Freeport, Maine
207-865-3004
Files for PCs, Macs, Amiga, Atari, and Apple

Homebuilt Flyer
Neenah, Wisconsin
414-725-7598
The meeting place for aviation enthusiasts

HouseNet
St Michaels, Maryland
410-745-2037
Tips for home repair and renovation

Arpeggio
Merion, Pennsylvania
215-667-7307
For musicians and lovers of all types of music

Botany Bay
Porthsmouth, New Hampshire
603-431-7229
Over 21 gigabytes of files

Writer's Block
South Bend, Indiana
219-232-2769
A place for writers to gather

AlterNet
Ashburnham, Massachusetts
508-827-5274
Focused on health and the environment

Missing Link
Waterloo, Iowa
39-235-0772
"When only the best is good enough"

Eagles Nest
Providence, Rhode Island
401-732-5292
A little something for everyone

The Polish Hideout
Teutopolis, Illinois
217-857-6370
First ever ethnic Polish-American, bilingual, BBS

Bear Waller Holler
Pikeville, Kentucky
606-437-4321
Good clean fun for the whole family

The Night Train
East Hartford, Connecticut
203-569-7978
Lots of on-line games and plenty of files

Origins Talk
Glendale, Missouri
314-821-1078
Discussing creation vs. evolution

Mindless One
Weirton, West Virginia
304-748-0491
Good friends and nice company

GLIB
Arlington, Virginia
703-578-4542
Information and news for the gay and lesbian community

The 3rd Eye
Nashville, Tennessee
615-227-1636
Serving couples and singles with an interest in the swinging lifestyle

The Vitamin Shop
Lumberton, New Jersey
609-778-5922
Focused on health, fitness, and nutrition

Mega Bytes
Lexington, North Carolina
704-744-6237
Specializes in desktop-publishing files

Arkansas River Valley
Russelville, Arkansas
501-968-1931
Home of InterNational Online Magazine

Leprechaun Castle
Carriere, Mississippi
601-799-2299
With 60 games on-line, can you find the pot o' gold?

The Final Decision
Atlanta, Georgia
404-876-0422
Fun and lots of files

Black Bag
Newark, Delaware
302-994-3772
Medical information and AIDS data

The Big Easy
New Orleans, Louisiana
504-827-5796
The "adult entertainment electroplex"

Galaxy
Clayhatchee, Alabama
205-598-9509
A free board from ACES, the Alabama Computer Enthusiasts Society

Time Travelers
Miami, Florida
305-256-3909
Home of the Worldwide Shareware Club

The Confederate States of America
Beaufort, South Carolina
803-846-8100
Lively debate of southern issues

ELECTRONIC MAIL

Electronic mail sounds like some kind of hot-wired, high-tech communications, but it's really not much different from any other kind of mail you receive. In simplest terms, electronic mail, or e-mail, is a message that is composed, addressed, and sent all with a computer. Like paper mail, e-mail can be courtesy copied to any number of individuals. It can be sent high-priority or with a return receipt. E-mail can be read, forwarded, replied to, printed, ignored, and thrown away. E-mail can even be translated from electronic form to paper form or fax and delivered via the U.S. Postal Service, overnight courier, or fax machine. Through your computer you can send messages to people around the world almost instantly. In short, e-mail is an extremely versatile communications medium.

E-mail is distinct from other on-line messages because it is delivered to a private mailbox, not posted for public view as are bulletin board and forum messages. As a member of an on-line service, including any of those mentioned in Chapter 8, you automatically get an electronic mailbox and your user ID serves as your address. Most bulletin board systems have e-mail services, too. Plus, there are a couple of on-line resources—such as MCI Mail and AT&T EasyLink—that do little more than provide e-mail services to the public.

E-MAIL BASICS

While the specifics of e-mail vary from service to service and bulletin board system to bulletin board system, there are some basic concepts that are similar across most all e-mail services. Typically, each e-mail message has four basic parts: the address, the subject, handling options (explained later in this section), and the message text. Sometimes, an e-mail message has an *attachment*—either an ASCII file or a binary file that is sent along with the message. Each e-mail message is marked with the date and time the message is sent and perhaps also an automatically generated identification number.

PARTS OF AN E-MAIL MESSAGE

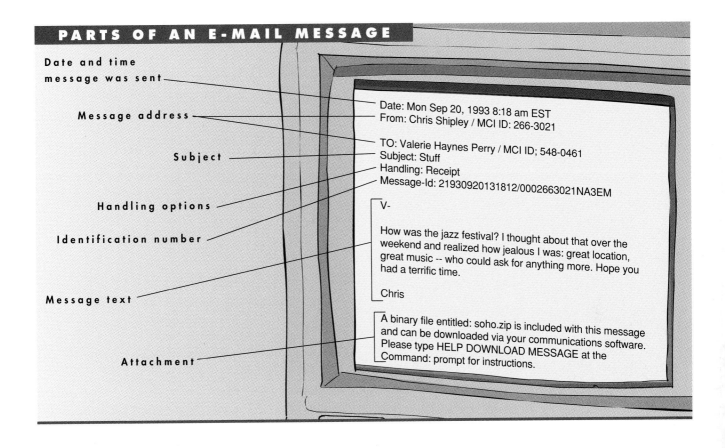

Date and time message was sent

Message address

Subject

Handling options

Identification number

Message text

Attachment

Date: Mon Sep 20, 1993 8:18 am EST
From: Chris Shipley / MCI ID: 266-3021

TO: Valerie Haynes Perry / MCI ID; 548-0461
Subject: Stuff
Handling: Receipt
Message-Id: 21930920131812/0002663021NA3EM

V-

How was the jazz festival? I thought about that over the weekend and realized how jealous I was: great location, great music -- who could ask for anything more. Hope you had a terrific time.

Chris

A binary file entitled: soho.zip is included with this message and can be downloaded via your communications software. Please type HELP DOWNLOAD MESSAGE at the Command: prompt for instructions.

The *address* is the part of the e-mail message where you designate the primary recipient and recipients of courtesy copies of your message. Many e-mail systems also let you create and name a mailing list that includes numerous recipients, and then send an e-mail message to everyone on the list by entering just the list name.

To address an e-mail message or create a mailing list, of course, you must know the address of the person or persons to whom you are sending e-mail. Most often, a person's user ID—either his or her name or an ID number—serves as the address. If you don't know the addressee's name as it appears on the service or in his or her ID, you can usually find it in an on-line directory of all service members. On CompuServe, for example, you access the member directory with the GO DIRECTORY command. On MCI Mail, one of the most popular public e-mail services, you enter FIND NAME at the command prompt. For example, you can easily look up the President's MCI Mail account as shown in the illustration Finding Someone on MCI Mail. Incidentally, the REMOTE in President Clinton's address indicates that his MCI Mail messages are automatically transferred from MCI Mail to the private e-mail system at the White House.

The *subject* of a message simply notes what the e-mail message is about. You can enter anything you like as the subject of your message or you can leave the subject field blank. It's always a good idea, though, to put *something* in the subject field as a courtesy to your recipient. This way, when recipients see the list of everything in their mailboxes, they can quickly tell what's important and read those messages first. The subject field might also indicate that a message is a reply to something you sent earlier or show that a message you sent with the return receipt handling option has been read by the addressee.

Handling options tell the e-mail service how you want your message to be sent. You may want, for example, to have the e-mail system notify you when the addressee receives your message, a common option called *return receipt*. Maybe your message is very important and should be sent high-priority so that it appears at the top of the recipients list of new messages. Some e-mail services offer special handling options that let you manage your outgoing mail in incredible detail, including specifying a charge code that appears on your bill and helps you track e-mail expenses on a per client or project basis. Most services also let you send your message via paper—either through the U.S. mail or by overnight courier—and you can even specify the letterhead and signature that appears on the page. Despite all these fancy options, however, most e-mail is sent without any special handling and simply sends the message from your out-box to the recipient's in-box.

NOTE *Every once in a while, you may get a message that has a return receipt attached. If you don't want the sender to know you've read the message, you can fool the system so the receipt is not returned to the sender. In MCI Mail, you do this by deleting the message, then scanning your trash and reading the message there. No return receipt is delivered to the sender.*

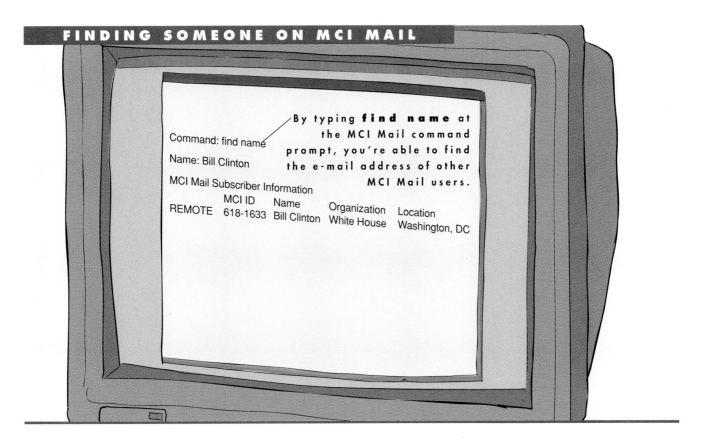

FINDING SOMEONE ON MCI MAIL

Command: find name

Name: Bill Clinton

MCI Mail Subscriber Information

By typing **find name** at the MCI Mail command prompt, you're able to find the e-mail address of other MCI Mail users.

	MCI ID	Name	Organization	Location
REMOTE	618-1633	Bill Clinton	White House	Washington, DC

Another way to play the same trick is to forward the message to youself and then read that copy of the message. This method may cost you the price of an e-mail message, but it preserves the original message in your mailbox so you can read it and send the receipt at a more appropriate time.

The *message text* is the heart of your e-mail message. You can enter your message by typing into the message area, or you can upload a text file as discussed in Chapter 7. E-mail messages can be short and sweet or long and complex—it's up to you. Some e-mail systems do have restrictions on the length of messages, but most simply charge more for longer messages. Many e-mail users, however, advocate keeping messages short because long-winded messages can be tedious to read on a computer screen. Furthermore, when writing to someone in e-mail, follow the same guidelines outlined in Chapter 2 for communicating clearly—for example, avoid typing messages in all capital

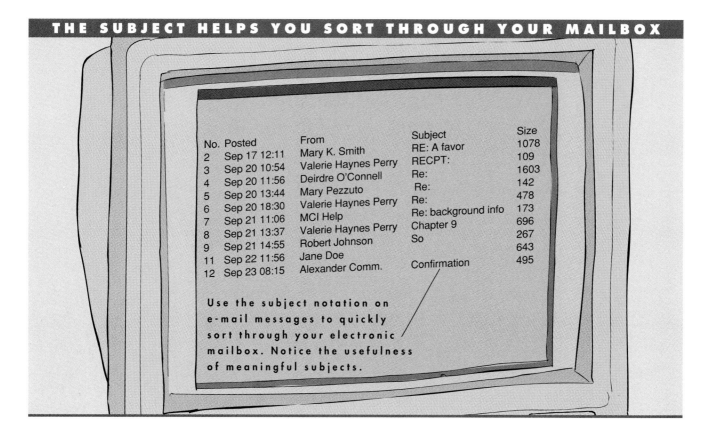

THE SUBJECT HELPS YOU SORT THROUGH YOUR MAILBOX

No.	Posted	From	Subject	Size
2	Sep 17 12:11	Mary K. Smith	RE: A favor	1078
3	Sep 20 10:54	Valerie Haynes Perry	RECPT:	109
4	Sep 20 11:56	Deirdre O'Connell	Re:	1603
5	Sep 20 13:44	Mary Pezzuto	Re:	142
6	Sep 20 18:30	Valerie Haynes Perry	Re:	478
7	Sep 21 11:06	MCI Help	Re: background info	173
8	Sep 21 13:37	Valerie Haynes Perry	Chapter 9	696
9	Sep 21 14:55	Robert Johnson	So	267
11	Sep 22 11:56	Jane Doe		643
12	Sep 23 08:15	Alexander Comm.	Confirmation	495

Use the subject notation on e-mail messages to quickly sort through your electronic mailbox. Notice the usefulness of meaningful subjects.

letters. In less formal communications, you may want to take advantage of emoticons and acronyms to keep your messages to the point.

An attachment is usually a binary file that is tagged onto an e-mail message, much as you might use a paper clip to attach a supporting document to a cover memo. Attached messages are uploaded to the e-mail service as part of the message and must be downloaded by the recipient in order to be used. An attachment can be a compressed file, a program file, or even a text file.

GETTING AROUND E-MAIL

Once you understand the basic components of an e-mail message, it's a snap to create one. Of course, each e-mail system works differently. In CompuServe Mail, for example, you COMPOSE a message. In MCI Mail you CREATE one. While the commands differ from service to service, usually the screen prompts or menus coach you to

RETURN RECEIPTS

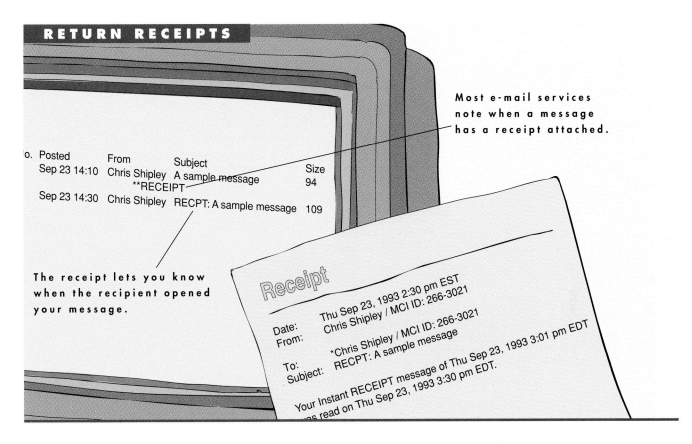

Most e-mail services note when a message has a receipt attached.

o. Posted	From	Subject	Size
Sep 23 14:10	Chris Shipley	A sample message **RECEIPT	94
Sep 23 14:30	Chris Shipley	RECPT: A sample message	109

The receipt lets you know when the recipient opened your message.

Receipt

Date: Thu Sep 23, 1993 2:30 pm EST
From: Chris Shipley / MCI ID: 266-3021

To: *Chris Shipley / MCI ID: 266-3021
Subject: RECPT: A sample message

Your Instant RECEIPT message of Thu Sep 23, 1993 3:01 pm EDT
was read on Thu Sep 23, 1993 3:30 pm EDT.

enter the addressee, the subject, and the message. Note, however, that some e-mail systems require you to write the message first and then enter the address information, while in others you must address the e-mail before you compose the message. Whether you prepare the message text before or after addressing it, you must indicate to the e-mail system that the message is complete when you've finished typing or uploading your message text. Again, each service uses a somewhat different indicator: CompuServe uses /exit to indicate the end of the message text, while MCI Mail uses just the slash (/) and a return as its end marker. After you've completed the message and the address, you choose special handling options if they are available, and use the service's command to send the message on its way.

Reading e-mail messages is just as easy as creating them. When you dial into a public e-mail service or log on to an on-line service, you will be told if you have new mail waiting for you. In most services, you scan your in-box to see a list of messages. The list will look a lot like the illustration The Subject Helps You Sort through Your Mailbox, earlier in this chapter. You'll see the date the message was sent, the sender's name, the subject, and the size of the message in bytes. Next to each message is a number that you use to refer to that message. To display a message, type **READ** and the message number (for example, **READ 1**) at the command prompt. Incidentally, SCAN and READ are the commands both MCI Mail and CompuServe mail use. Other e-mail services may use slightly different commands.

When you are finished reading a message you can reply usually by entering a command such as **REPLY** or **ANSWER**. The e-mail service automatically addresses the reply to the sender of the original message, notes the subject as a response to the original subject, and waits for you to enter the message text. When you reply, you can choose to reply only to the sender or to the sender and all other people who may have received a copy of the original message. You can also forward the message to another person, using a forward command. The e-mail service attaches a copy of the original message to a new message. You simply fill in the address and add any comment you like to the message area. And, of course, you can delete messages to keep mail from cluttering up your in-box.

Most major e-mail systems provide a fax option that enables you to compose an e-mail message and fax it to any fax machine anywhere in the world. This option is great when you want to send the same message to a number of people, some who have e-mail addresses and others who do not have e-mail addresses but can be reached by fax. To send a fax through MCI Mail, for example, you address the message as shown in the illustration Sending a Fax through E-mail.

E-mail-to-fax messages are a lifesaver when you don't have a printer, but you need a hard copy of something on your computer. You can use the e-mail system to fax the text to a nearby fax machine and voilà—hard copy.

SENDING A FAX THROUGH E-MAIL

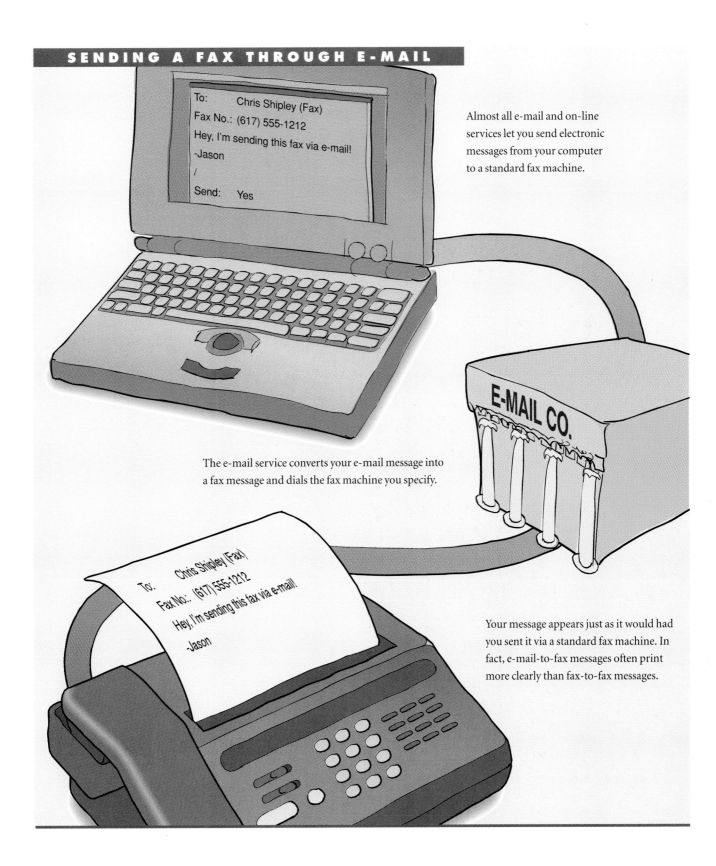

To: Chris Shipley (Fax)
Fax No.: (617) 555-1212
Hey, I'm sending this fax via e-mail!
-Jason
/
Send: Yes

Almost all e-mail and on-line services let you send electronic messages from your computer to a standard fax machine.

The e-mail service converts your e-mail message into a fax message and dials the fax machine you specify.

E-MAIL CO.

To: Chris Shipley (Fax)
Fax No.: (617) 555-1212
Hey, I'm sending this fax via e-mail!
-Jason

Your message appears just as it would had you sent it via a standard fax machine. In fact, e-mail-to-fax messages often print more clearly than fax-to-fax messages.

E-MAIL AND ON-LINE SERVICES

I f you belong to an on-line service, then you already have access to e-mail. Each major commercial on-line service provides e-mail services to its members. Here, again, each service differs somewhat, both in the scope of its capabilities and the way it works. While the specific details are rather mundane, a brief overview here of the e-mail offered by the "Big Three" on-line services—America Online, CompuServe, and Prodigy—may help you choose which of these services you'd like to use.

America Online has expanded its intermember mail service to include e-mail access to services outside of America Online. Through e-mail, you can send fax and U.S. mail, and you can send electronic messages to virtually any other e-mail system. (More on how that works later in this chapter.) Although you can't attach files to messages sent from America Online to other e-mail services, messages between America Online members can include attachments. America Online has a messaging option called Instant Message, which allows you to write a brief note to another member who is logged on to the service. Your message appears immediately on the recipient's screen. If you don't want to be bothered by notes popping up on screen, you can choose to block this feature so that no one can send you an Instant Message. E-mail services are charged at the standard connect time rates. Fax and paper mail cost an additional $2.00 and $2.50, respectively.

CompuServe Mail is by far the most widely used e-mail service among those offered by the major on-line services. In fact, many people sign up for CompuServe *just* to use the e-mail system. In addition to the typical array of e-mail services, CompuServe Mail offers a number of special features such as Congressgram, which enables you to send a message to members of the Congress. Like America Online, CompuServe Mail provides access to other e-mail systems, too. E-mail prices are based on the size of the message, counted in blocks of 2,500 characters. Each block costs $.05 with a minimum $.15 charge. Additional fees are levied for return receipts and other options. The basic CompuServe membership fee includes a monthly "allowance" of $9.00 worth of e-mail services, enough to cover about 60 three-page messages in either text or binary form. Some special services are not included in the monthly allowance.

Prodigy, until recently, had the most limited of the on-line service e-mail systems. It was great for sending messages to other Prodigy members, but messages could be no more than six screen lengths. You couldn't attach files to messages. There was no option to send e-mail to other on-line services, nor could you send a message via fax or paper mail. Prodigy has started to change all that. In the fall of 1993, the service began testing a new Mail Manager utility to offer Prodigy members the same e-mail options found on other services. The utility, along with links to outside services, was expected to be in place by the time this book is available. Up to 30 messages are included in the monthly membership fee and connect time charges are suspended while reading and writing messages.

COMMERCIAL E-MAIL SERVICES

In addition to the e-mail systems provided by commercial on-line services, there are a few major commercial e-mail services that might be thought of as large electronic post offices. When you sign up with one of these services, you are given a mailbox, just as if you rented a P.O. box from the U.S. post office in your town. The commercial e-mail service lets you exchange e-mail with other people who have mailboxes on the service and with people on other e-mail services, just as the commercial on-line services do. The difference between commercial on-line services and commercial e-mail services is that the latter offer little other than mail service. The two largest commercial e-mail services are MCI Mail and AT&T Mail. The decision to sign up for a commercial e-mail service depends on your answer to one key question: Do you communicate regularly enough with other people who also use the service? These commercial e-mail services are great for business communications, but may not be as cost-effective as the e-mail services provided by an on-line service you already use.

MCI Mail is perhaps the more popular commercial e-mail service. Using MCI Mail, you can send a message to virtually anyone in the world. If you address a message to someone who is not also an MCI Mail patron, the service gives you the option of addressing a letter, which the e-mail system will then print and mail to the recipient. If overland mail isn't fast enough, you can have your message delivered by overnight courier or fax, instead. MCI Mail has one neat handling option that's a big help for people who must track their communications. Using the handling option CHARGE, you can assign each message a project code that will be referenced on your MCI billing statement. MCI will keep a copy of your letterhead on file to use when you send paper mail through the service, and can even add your digitized signature to the bottom of the page. Prices are based on the size of the message. The first 500 characters cost $.50, the second are an additional $.10. From there, charges are levied in 1,000 character blocks, costing $.10 each up to 10,000 characters, then $.05 for each additional 1,000 characters. Additional fees are charged for paper and fax services. You can contact MCI Mail at 800-444-6245 or 202-833-8484.

AT&T Mail offers a range of message services, including fax, telex, paper delivery, and, of course, e-mail. While marketed primarily to very large companies, the service can be purchased by individuals, and AT&T is working on a new consumer service to be launched some time in 1994. Even though you can access AT&T Mail through any communications software, AT&T Mail Access PLUS software (for Windows, DOS, and Macintosh personal computers) makes the job much easier. There is a registration fee of $3.00 per month plus message fees based on 1,000 character units. The first 1,000 characters cost $.50, the next 1,000 are an additional $.30, and the third 1,000 an additional $.15. All additional 1,000 character blocks are $.05 cents. You can contact AT&T Mail at 800-242-6005 or 201-331-4000.

SENDING E-MAIL FROM ONE SERVICE TO ANOTHER

Each e-mail service—whether part of an on-line service, a commercial e-mail service, or even a bulletin board system—has its own way of handling electronic mail. They all work great when e-mail is being sent to other members of the same service. But the differences also serve to make each service an island, unable to communicate with others. To combat this problem, a group of international communications specialists established a standard method of exchanging e-mail between services. The standard, known generally as Message Handling Systems (MHS), describes how messages are to be passed from one service to another across what is commonly called a *gateway*. So long as the e-mail service you use has a gateway, you can send messages to people who use other services.

Using the Internet as a Gateway   Most e-mail services use the *Internet* as their gateway. The Internet is a connection of networks spanning the globe. Born of a partnership between the U.S. Department of Defense and a number of American universities, the Internet was a means of connecting computers around the country so that people could share information with one another. Today, it is an information superhighway connecting hundreds of thousands of computer systems, including the major commercial on-line and e-mail services and many public bulletin board systems.

When you send a message from your e-mail service to someone on another system, that message likely will travel across the Internet to reach its destination. The only trick, though, is addressing the message properly so that the Internet knows where to deliver it.

In simplest terms, an Internet address consists of two parts. First, you must know the recipient's name or ID on his or her home service, and you must follow the name with the @ symbol. Second, you need the Internet name of the e-mail system to which you are sending the message. These names are followed by a suffix describing the type of organization. Once you know the address of your friends and associates and the e-mail service they use, you can send messages to them just as if they were on your home e-mail service.

Here is a list of Internet suffixes:

▶ *.COM—businesses and commercial services, such as CompuServe and America Online*

▶ *.EDU—schools and universities*

▶ *.GOV—government agencies*

▶ *.MIL—military installations*

▶ *.ORG—noncommercial, nonnetwork sites and gateways, such as bulletin board systems*

▶ *.NET—networks that link to the Internet*

In addition to knowing Internet suffixes, you should also be aware of the Internet names for the most popular on-line services:

aol.com	America Online
compuserve.com	CompuServe
delphi.com	Delphi
genie.geis.com	GEnie
prodigy.com	Prodigy
attmail.com	AT&T Mail
mcimail.com	MCI Mail

Lastly, here is a sample Internet address:

`CSHIPLEY@mcimail.com`

for my MCI Mail address, or

`76000.16@compuserve.com`

for my CompuServe Mail address.

E-MAIL SERVICES ARE LINKED THROUGH GATEWAYS

You can send a message from one e-mail system to another through gateways that bridge services. Because it is so widely used, the Internet system of electronic networks is most often used as that gateway.

To send a message from one service to another, you must know the address your recipient uses on his or her home service, plus the Internet address of the recipient's home service.

E-mail systems typically use an Internet address consisting of the name of the service followed by a .COM extension. For example, compuserve.com for CompuServe, aol.com for America Online, genie.geis.com for GEnie, and so forth.

EXTRA!

ZiffNet

A WORLD OF INFORMATION

News, Sports, and Weather

A Reference Library On Line

Travel Services

That's Entertainment

11

It is hard to imagine a conventional library with holdings in books, magazines, and other periodicals as vast and up to date as the amounts of information available to people who go on line. The enormous information resources on line are not only hard to imagine, but also impossible to outline in one chapter of a book. Instead, this chapter is a whirlwind tour of only some of the information resources available on line. Suffice it to say, this is just the tip of the information iceberg.

NEWS, SPORTS, AND WEATHER

News junkies can get no better fix than the news they'll get on line. Provided by the same national and international news agencies that supply the major media—Associated Press, Reuters, UPI, and USA Today, among others—on-line news is brought to you as the stories break. In most cases, the day's news is updated hourly, but big stories are often monitored minute-to-minute. On election day in November 1992, for example, Prodigy posted election returns as they were reported state-by-state. During major national disasters, such as the San Francisco Bay Area earthquake and Hurricane Andrew, on-line news was in some cases the only way people learned of the fates of family and friends. All the major on-line services and many bulletin board systems provide some coverage of the day's top stories, and a few even provide customized news services and in-depth coverage via relationships with specific news agencies.

All the news is great for news fanatics, but what if you just want to find out more about a specific story, or you care to follow only a few issues. Because some on-line services save news stories in a database, you can search for past articles to find out more about a specific topic. In addition to these news archives, some on-line services let you specify your news needs, and then receive only the stories that match your interests. Here are some of the customized news services you'll find on line:

GEnie QuikNews (GEnie, keyword QUICKNEWS) and **Executive News Service** (CompuServe, GO ENS) are electronic clipping services that deliver to you exactly the stories you want to read. You design your news profile by specifying a number of searches and choosing the regular columns and features you want to receive. The on-line service scans all incoming news material, finds those stories that match your profile, and delivers them to your electronic mailbox.

Newspaper Library (CompuServe, GO NEWSLIB) and **Newsstand** (GEnie keyword NEWSSTAND) are searchable databases of selected full-text articles from dozens of newspapers across the United States. The database includes major metropolitan daily papers, such as the *Atlanta Journal Constitution*, the *Boston Globe*, the *Chicago Tribune*, the *Los Angeles Times*, and the *Miami Herald*, as well as some smaller papers, including the *Akron Beacon Journal* (Ohio), the *Fresno Bee* (California), and the *Lexington Herald-Leader* (Kentucky).

NewsWatch (America Online, keyword NEWSWATCH) and **NewsGrid** (CompuServe, GO NEWSGRID) enable you to find specific, current news stories related to the search words or phrases you specify. These news databases include thousands of stories from the world's leading wire services and include U.S. and world news headlines, business news headlines, stock market and economic updates, and hundreds of general news stories. Every two minutes, approximately one new story is added to these databases by the Comtex News Service.

More and more news-related organizations are realizing that they can reach a broader audience with more current and different kinds of information by bringing their services on line, rather than limiting themselves to newspapers or even television

WHERE TO FIND NEWS, SPORTS, AND WEATHER

These lists will give you a head start at finding the news, sports, and weather information available on the following on-line services.

America Online

Resource	Keyword
Business and financial news	business
CNN Newsroom	cnn
News search	newswatch
TIME Magazine Online	time
Top news stories	top news
USA Today Decisionline	usatoday
Sports news	sports
Hurricane Center	hurricanes
Weather forecasts	weather

CompuServe

Resource	Go Word
AP Online	APO
The Business Wire	TBW
Dow Jones News/Retrieval	DJ
Executive News Service	ENS
NewsGrid	NEWSGRID
Newspaper Library	NEWSLIB
Reuter NewsPictures	NEWSPIX
UK News Clips	UKNEWS
AP Sports Wire	APSPORTS
UK weather forecasts	UKWEATHER

GEnie

Resource	Keyword
Dow Jones News/Retrieval	DOWJONES
Newsbytes	NEWSBYTES
Newstand	NEWSTAND
QuikNews	QUICKNEWS
Reuters Newswires	REUTERS
US & World News	NEWS
Ski conditions	TRAVEL

Prodigy

Resource	Jump Word
Business news	business news
Economic news	economic up
Top news stories	headlines
Sports news	sports news
Ski conditions	ski center
US City forecasts	w us cities

ZiffNet

Resource	Go Word
MacWeek news	ZMC:NEWSMAC
Newsbytes	NEWSBYTES
PC Week news	PCWNEWS

broadcasts. Several newspapers, news weeklies, and television broadcast companies are finding they can deliver the stories that didn't make it to the printed page by coming on line. They can also provide downloadable files that enhance stories and talk directly to their readers and viewers through electronic mail and bulletin boards. These are just a few of the news agencies who have brought their reporting skills on line:

CNN Newsroom (America Online, keyword CNN) is not just a news service, it's also an educational resource, a discussion forum, and a library of multimedia news clips. A project of Turner Broadcasting's Turner Educational Services, Inc., the CNN Newsroom is a 15-minute television news program that highlights the top stories of the day and presents student interest segments and daily special features. The program is supplemented by a Classroom Guide designed to enhance classroom learning about current events.

Dow Jones News/Retrieval (CompuServe, GO DJ; GEnie, keyword DOWJONES; MCI Mail, //BUSINESS; for information about direct access through Dow Jones call 609-452-1511) is one of the oldest news services covering the news that affects stock prices. The service reports on U.S. and international stock markets, company information, and market-affecting economic and political news.

Newsbytes (America Online, keyword NEWSBYTES; CompuServe, GO NEWS-BYTES; ZiffNet, GO NEWSBYTES, GEnie, keyword NEWSBYTES) is an international news service covering high technology. Newsbytes provides 30 to 40 stories each weekday, covering the significant developments in personal computing, telecommunications, microprocessors, and other technologies.

Reuter NewsPictures Forum (CompuServe, GO NEWSPIX) provides the pictures that go with the news stories. The forum contains news photos in .GIF format that can be viewed while you are connected to CompuServe or downloaded and viewed off line. In addition to current news photos, the forum's Bettmann Archives includes photos of historical importance.

TIME Online (America Online, keyword TIME), an experiment between *TIME* magazine and America Online, provides text of the current issue of *TIME*, plus some of the stories that didn't make it into the magazine because of space limitations and late-breaking news. You can also search past issues, discuss current events with other America Online members, send letters to the editor for publication, or subscribe to *TIME* magazine for home delivery.

USA Today and **USA Today Decisionline** (America Online, keyword USA-TODAY; also available through many bulletin board systems and directly from USA Today—for access number call 800-826-9688) provide news summaries on line each morning by 7 a.m. eastern time.

But there's more to news than the local and national beats. You also have access to the latest sports scores, league standings, and game schedules for most professional sporting events and for many college sports, too. On line is the perfect place for the armchair athlete. You'll find the latest news from the world of sports, plus scores, stats, schedules and more. And if you'd rather talk about sports than play them, there are plenty of discussion forums to choose from. All the major services offer sports news and discussions, and there's even one specialty sports service:

USA Today Sports Center (for local access number call 800-826-9688) is the sports lover's dream come true. The center updates stats daily for individual players in the major leagues and weekly for players in the minors, and it also provides game scores and team standings. It even has a Fantasy Sports League where you can manage your own football, baseball, or basketball team. You draft and trade players from the pro sports rosters, and then compete against other Sports Center members around the world.

And who wants to sit in the rain to watch a baseball game? Before you head out to the old ball yard—or just about anywhere else—you'll want to check the weather forecast. Every major on-line service and many bulletin board systems provide reports for local, national, and international locations, along with the same weather maps you see on the six o'clock news. Of course, there are some specialty reports, too.

Hurricane Center (America Online, keyword HURRICANE) tracks the development of tropical storms and hurricanes throughout the hurricane season. In addition to downloading color maps tracking these storms and reading the Hurricane Watch bulletins, members are encouraged to exchange information and tips in the Hurricane Message Center.

Ski reports (Prodigy, JUMP SKI CENTER; GEnie, keyword TRAVEL) give the weather and slope conditions at resorts across the United States and Canada. You'll also find information on resorts, lodgings, and other recreation and entertainment at major alpine and cross-country ski destinations.

Weather maps (America Online, keyword WEATHER; CompuServe, GO WEATHER; Prodigy, JUMP WEATHER) provide in one picture a quick summary of the day's forecast. Each service provides a different range of maps. All give basic weather pattern maps, and America Online and CompuServe also provide radar maps, jet stream maps, and other maps that can be downloaded and viewed off line.

A REFERENCE LIBRARY ON LINE

It's hard to think of a question that can't be answered on line. It's harder still to imagine being satisfied with the answer to just one question when there are so many information resources to search through. If you think there's a lot of news on line, just wait until you start exploring the gigantic reference libraries. For example, the Library of Congress (America Online, keyword: LIBRARY OF CONGRESS) is represented on line through a pilot program intended to make the public more aware of the library, its purpose, and its resources. This on-line resource provides historical information about the library as well as brief descriptions of the public services that the library has to offer, including, where available, phone numbers, addresses, or even electronic mailboxes where more information can be obtained. It also features information about the library's special exhibits and services, including the American Folklife Center, The National Library Service for the Blind and Physically Handicapped, and special visiting installations.

REFERENCE RESOURCES

You'll find entire libraries of reference material on line.

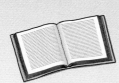

America Online

Resource	Keyword
Academic Assistance Center	homework
Compton's Encyclopedia	encyclopedia
	comptons
Computer terms dictionary	computerterms
Consumer Reports	consumer reports
Employer contacts database	contacts
National Geographic Online	geographic

CompuServe

Resource	Go Word
Books in Print	BOOKS
Census Bureau data	CENDATA
College database	PETERSON
Consumer Reports	CONSUMER
Health database	HNT
Legal research center	LEGALRC
Magazine database	MAGDB
Marquis Who's Who	BIOGRAPHY
Phone listings	PHONEFILE or BIZFILE
Trademark Research Center	TRADERC

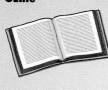

GEnie

Resource	Keyword
College financial aid sources	CASHE
Company profiles	D&BPROFILES
GEnie Reference Center	REFCENTER
Magazine database	NEWSSTAND
Patent database	PATENTS
PhotoSource International	PSI
Research and reference services	RESEARCH or REFERENCE
Thomas Register of US manufactures	TRESISTER
Trademark registration database	TRADEMARKS

Prodigy

Resource	Jump Word
Consumer Reports	consumer reports
Encyclopedia	encyclopedia
Parenting information	parenting

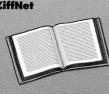

ZiffNet

Resource	Go Word
Business database	BUSDB
Computer books	BOOKNET
Computer periodicals database	COMPLIB
Computer product directory	COMPDIR
Health database	HEALTHDB
Magazine database	MAGDB
Technical support database	ONSITE

On-line dictionaries, encyclopedias, and directories are more current than their hardback counterparts because they can be regularly updated to reflect the changing world. They also make it very easy to search for the information you want, and their cross-referencing features help you find additional material related to your topic. You'll find an encyclopedia or dictionary on every on-line service. There are also specialty directories; here's a small sampling:

Biz*File (CompuServe, GO BIZFILE) lists over 10 million U.S. and Canadian businesses, including business name, address, phone number, and length of time the particular business has been listed in the yellow pages. You can search Biz*File by company name, company phone number, and by the type of business.

Peterson's College Database (CompuServe, GO PETERSON) contains descriptions of over 3,400 accredited U.S. and Canadian colleges that grant associate's and bachelor's degrees. You can search the database by a variety of criteria, such as special majors, cost, location, financial aid, and athletics.

Phone*File (CompuServe, GO PHONEFILE) is a database of over 80 million U.S. households, and it contains consumer data including name, home address, phone number, and length of residence. The information contained in Phone*File is obtained from public records or published information. You can search the listing by name, zip code, city, state, or phone number.

The Thomas Register (GEnie, keyword TREGISTER) lets you find manufacturers of specific products by searching for a type of product. The register includes manufacturers in North America and lists them by name or by product.

Webster's Dictionary of Computer Terms (America Online, keyword COMPUTERTERMS) keeps you current on the lingo of the computer business. The dictionary includes more than 4,500 terms to help you distinguish your bits from your bytes. In addition to defining the jargon, it also includes helpful descriptions of major software programs.

There are stacks and stacks of periodicals—magazines, professional journals, newsletters, and more—all available in electronic form. Many of these publications are provided in *full-text*, meaning once you find an article that meets your search criteria, you can retrieve it and read the entire piece on line or download it to your computer. And often, years' worth of publications are stored electronically, so you can find historical and reference information for a variety of purposes.

Consumer Reports (America Online, keyword CONSUMER REPORTS; CompuServe GO CONSUMER; Prodigy, JUMP CONSUMER REPORTS) provides reviews and reports prepared by the Consumers Union and modified somewhat from their print form to accommodate on-line searching. Most services carry reports in categories such as appliances, automobiles, and electronics.

DIALOG (Delphi; contact 800-334-2564 to access directly from DIALOG Information Service) is a gigantic database of articles from leading newspapers, wire services, periodicals, reference works, magazines, journals, and newsletters. Actually, DIALOG is more than 450 databases containing over 330 million articles, abstracts, and citations. DIALOG is the source for many other on-line research services, but it can also be accessed directly.

IQuest (CompuServe, GO IQUEST) is a comprehensive information and reference service with access to over 800 publications, databases, and indexes spanning the worlds of business, government, research, news, entertainment, and sports. IQuest is a menu-based service; it prompts you for your information needs and then conducts a search by accessing various on-line database services. The service returns a list of up to 10 bibliographic references and 15 full-text titles, from which you select articles to be retrieved. While IQuest is a comprehensive service, it can carry significant costs depending on the databases it searches and the articles it retrieves.

Knowledge Index (CompuServe, GO KI) provides evening and weekend access to over 100 popular full-text and bibliographic databases at reduced rates. The service covers more than 50,000 journals on a wide variety of topics, including business and finance publications, engineering and technical articles, medical journals, and law publications.

Lexis and Nexis (contact Mead Data Central at 800-227-4908 or at 800-227-8379 in Ohio) are the leading full-text information services for the legal and business communities, respectively. An archive of federal and state case law, Lexis has 45 libraries covering all major fields of legal practice. Nexis provides full-text articles from more than 1,000 news publications, and is the exclusive source of the *New York Times* archives on line.

The Librarian (Delphi) is available to Delphi members who would rather not wade through the on-line research services themselves. Ask any question, and the answer is researched by information specialists at Searchline Associates in Brookline Massachusetts. The answer is selected from an on-line retrieval system that summarizes 3,000 journals, magazines, newspapers, and directories. A customized literature search is delivered to your Delphi mailbox—costs rage from $275.00 to $475.00.

Magazine Database Plus (CompuServe, GO MAGDB) and **Newsstand** (GEnie, keyword NEWSSTAND) let you retrieve full-text articles from hundreds of general-interest magazines, journals, and reports. The database contains a wealth of diverse publications, from popular glossy magazines to weeklies and special-interest publications.

You'll find a complete medical library available through a number of on-line services. These libraries contain articles from hundreds of medical journals and concise dictionaries of health and medical information.

CAIN: The Computerized AIDS Information Network (Delphi) provides the latest information about AIDS research, treatment, and prevention. It also serves as a forum for caregivers and people with AIDS and AIDS-related illnesses to discuss their treatments and provide support for one another.

The HealthNet Reference Library (CompuServe, GO HNT; Delphi) is a complete source of health and medical information. It is concise yet comprehensive enough to answer most health-related questions. You can search the library by disease, symptom, drug, and so on, or you can browse the library by starting with one topic and following the trail of related articles on the subject.

Travel Services

After all that news and research, it's time to relax and have some fun. Does it come as any surprise that you'll find plenty of resources for travel information on line? Before you hit the road, it's a good idea to check the recommendations of your fellow travelers who are more than happy to share their views in on-line discussion forums. On-line services often post foreign exchange rates, State Department Travel Advisories, and customs and passport regulations. You'll also find electronic versions of popular travel guides, including the Mobil Travel Guides (Prodigy, JUMP MOBIL) and the Zagat's Restaurant Surveys (CompuServe, GO ZAGAT; Prodigy, JUMP ZAGAT). In addition to these well-known travel guides, there are several other helpful directories and forums:

ABC Worldwide Hotel Guide (CompuServe, GO ABC) provides comprehensive listings of over 60,000 hotel properties worldwide. The directory includes information on each hotel, the street address, location information (distance from downtown), local and toll-free telephone numbers, fax numbers, telex numbers, number of rooms, hotel facilities (in-room, in-hotel, sports and leisure), business services, and credit cards accepted.

Adventure Atlas (GEnie, keyword TRAVEL) lets you match your travel and leisure interests with hundreds of trips and adventures. You respond to questions about what you like, when you want to travel, and what areas you'd like to visit, and Adventure Atlas suggests trips that meet your criteria.

Bed and Breakfast Guide Online (America Online, keyword BED & BREAK-FAST) is the electronic version of *The Complete Guide to Bed and Breakfasts, Inns and Guest Houses in the United States and Canada,* by Pamela Lanier. This on-line guide includes listings of over 9,000 beds-and-breakfasts and small inns in the United States and Canada.

RESOURCES FOR TRAVELERS

Don't leave home before checking on-line travel resources.

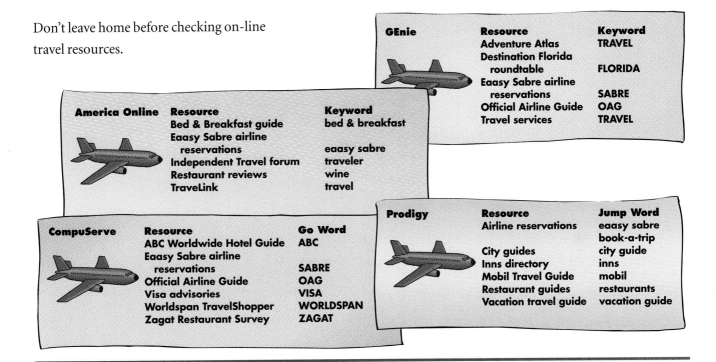

America Online	Resource	Keyword
	Bed & Breakfast guide	bed & breakfast
	Eaasy Sabre airline reservations	eaasy sabre
	Independent Travel forum	traveler
	Restaurant reviews	wine
	TraveLink	travel

GEnie	Resource	Keyword
	Adventure Atlas	TRAVEL
	Destination Florida roundtable	FLORIDA
	Eaasy Sabre airline reservations	SABRE
	Official Airline Guide	OAG
	Travel services	TRAVEL

CompuServe	Resource	Go Word
	ABC Worldwide Hotel Guide	ABC
	Eaasy Sabre airline reservations	SABRE
	Official Airline Guide	OAG
	Visa advisories	VISA
	Worldspan TravelShopper	WORLDSPAN
	Zagat Restaurant Survey	ZAGAT

Prodigy	Resource	Jump Word
	Airline reservations	eaasy sabre book-a-trip
	City guides	city guide
	Inns directory	inns
	Mobil Travel Guide	mobil
	Restaurant guides	restaurants
	Vacation travel guide	vacation guide

City Guides (Prodigy, jump CITY GUIDES) were developed from member surveys and provide listings of local restaurants, lodgings, and entertainment for major U.S. cities, including Atlanta, Boston, Chicago, Dallas, Las Vegas, Los Angeles, San Francisco, Philadelphia, Miami, and New York. You'll also find guides for Florida, Hawaii, and London.

Goldwyn's DineBase (America Online, keyword WINE) contains the 1,200 top-rated restaurants throughout the United States. All are recommended by one or more prestigious review organizations, among them AAA Dining Award, DiRoNA, Mobil Frequent Traveler's Guide to Major Cities, Restaurant Hospitality Wine List Awards, Wine Spectator's Great Restaurant Wine Lists, and Zagat Restaurant Surveys.

The Independent Traveler (America Online, keyword TRAVELER) is a travel forum primarily geared to people who enjoy the fun and adventure of traveling independently. The forum is a great place for sharing tales and advice from your own travels and for finding tips about the best places to go on your next trip.

Inns Directory (Prodigy, JUMP INNS) is a searchable listing of small inns and bed-and-breakfasts throughout the United States. The listings are provided and paid for by owners of the establishments and are not endorsed by the on-line service.

Just looking up information on your travel destination is useful, but the really valuable services are making your airline, hotel, and car rental reservations directly on line. Here are the most popular services available:

Eaasy Sabre (America Online, keyword EAASY SABRE; CompuServe, GO SABRE; GEnie, keyword SABRE; Prodigy, JUMP EAASY SABRE) is an airline, car rental, and hotel reservation system, based on the comprehensive reservation system used by airlines and travel agents. Eaasy Sabre lists the availability for over 600 airlines, 18,000 hotels worldwide, and over 45 car rental companies. You can use the service to book and confirm reservations and purchase airline tickets on 300 air carriers.

The Official Airline Guides Electronic Edition (CompuServe, GO OAG; GEnie, keyword OAG) is a comprehensive, up-to-date source of travel-related information, including lodging information, flight schedules, airline fares, and actual seat availability. You can use the guide to book flights and have tickets delivered to your home or office. In addition to airline information, the guide provides travel news and information about discount travel packages.

WorldSpan TravelShopper (CompuServe, GO WORLDSPAN) lets you shop for the best airfare to meet your itinerary. You'll get a complete listing of all available flights on all airlines that accommodate your travel plans, including a list of fares for each flight.

THAT'S ENTERTAINMENT

If your kind of relaxing happens closer to home, you'll find plenty to keep you entertained on line. Couch potatoes can get the latest reviews, ratings, and gossip about their favorite television programs on just about any on line service. Daytime TV fans don't have to worry about missing an episode of their favorite soap; the major on-line services all offer soap opera summaries to keep you up to date. If you prefer a darkened theater,

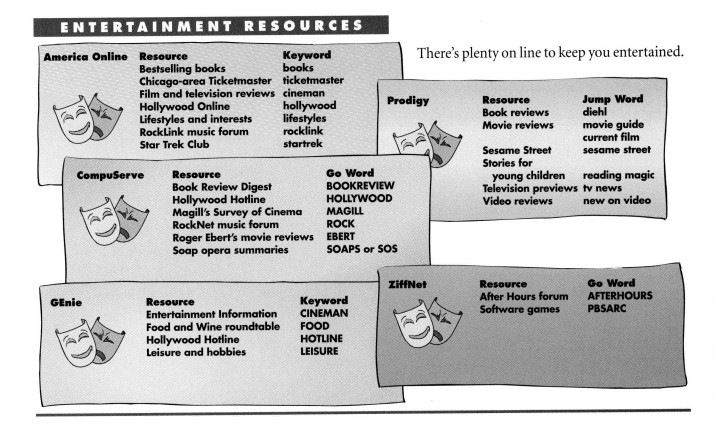

ENTERTAINMENT RESOURCES

There's plenty on line to keep you entertained.

America Online

Resource	Keyword
Bestselling books	books
Chicago-area Ticketmaster	ticketmaster
Film and television reviews	cineman
Hollywood Online	hollywood
Lifestyles and interests	lifestyles
RockLink music forum	rocklink
Star Trek Club	startrek

Prodigy

Resource	Jump Word
Book reviews	diehl
Movie reviews	movie guide
	current film
Sesame Street Stories for	sesame street
young children	reading magic
Television previews	tv news
Video reviews	new on video

CompuServe

Resource	Go Word
Book Review Digest	BOOKREVIEW
Hollywood Hotline	HOLLYWOOD
Magill's Survey of Cinema	MAGILL
RockNet music forum	ROCK
Roger Ebert's movie reviews	EBERT
Soap opera summaries	SOAPS or SOS

ZiffNet

Resource	Go Word
After Hours forum	AFTERHOURS
Software games	PBSARC

GEnie

Resource	Keyword
Entertainment Information	CINEMAN
Food and Wine roundtable	FOOD
Hollywood Hotline	HOTLINE
Leisure and hobbies	LEISURE

you'll find plenty of movie reviews, coming attractions, and cinema trivia on most services, too. To really stay on top of show business, though, check out some of these services:

Cineman Syndicate (America Online, keyword CINEMAN; Delphi; GEnie, keyword ENTERTAIN) provides a library of capsule reviews of the latest films, weekly box-office reports, video reviews, coming attractions, book reviews, and data about practically anything else coming out of the entertainment industry.

Hollywood Online (America Online, keyword HOLLYWOOD) features sneak previews of the hottest new motion pictures. You can download multimedia previews and pictures of your favorite stars from the Pictures and Sounds library, read about the cast and production notes in Movie Notes, and talk about the movies on the Movie Talk message board.

Hollywood Hotline (CompuServe, GO HOLLYWOOD; Delphi; GEnie, keyword ENTERTAINMENT) brings you daily entertainment news, along with an encyclopedia of entertainment information. You'll find prime-time TV schedules, a calendar of celebrity birthdays, records of Academy, Tony, and Grammy Award winners, and a complete history of The Beatles' tours.

Magill's Survey of Cinema (CompuServe, GO MAGILL) is a movie lover's resource. The database has information on more than 30,000 films released since 1902, including each film's title, release information, cast and credits, plot summary, and other related information.

Penn & Teller (Delphi), the outrageous magic act that describes itself as "two eccentric guys who have learned to do a few cool things," have brought their New-York-City-based bulletin board, known as MOFO ex Machina, to Delphi. It's a place to talk about magic and madness, follow their tour schedule, and learn a few of their wacky secrets.

News, sports, weather, research, travel, and entertainment. These are just a very few of the things you'll find on line. If I tried to catalog all the information resources available on line, this chapter would go on for hundreds of pages and make only a small dent in the number of available resources. As you explore on-line services, you'll doubtless find hundreds of resources I have yet to discover. Hopefully, you'll locate the one or two information outlets that exactly meet your needs.

MISCELLANEOUS TOPICS

Now that you've become acquainted with
using keywords to access specific resources,
here are a few more keyword boxes containing
some miscellaneous topics.

GEnie Resource	Go Word
Adventures of the hi-tech nomad	NOMAD
Astrology news and events	ASTRO
Classified ads	ADS
Game room	GAMES
Help with GEnie	HELP
Macintosh product support	MAC-PS
Musicians roundtable	MUSIC
On-line loan calculator	LOAN
Super Bowl pool	SUPERBOWL

America Online Resource	Keyword
Astronomy Club	astronomy
Casino games	casino
Center Stage Auditorium	centerstage
College board on line	college board
disABILITIES forum	disabilities
Ethics and religion forum	religion
Fight Back with David Horowitz	fightback
Help with America Online	ask aol
Job listing database	jobs
Romance connection	romance
Writer's Club	writers

Prodigy Resource	Jump Word
Babysitters Club	bsc
Educational software	schoolware, ziff selections
Fantasy baseball game	baseball man
Macintosh computer expert	rosenthal
Science for kids	nova
Service help	help hub
Stores on line	power shop
Stories for children	reading magic

CompuServe Resource	Go Word
AIDS information	AIDS
Bacchus Wine forum	WINEFORUM
Chess players forum	CHESSFORUM
CongressGram	CONGRESS
The Electronic Mall	MALL
Gardening forum	GARDENING
Government publications	GPO
Help with CompuServe	HELPFORUM
NCAA Collegiate Sports network	NCAA
New car showroom	NEWCAR
Sports medicine information	INFOUSA

ZiffNet Resource	Go Word
Computer Library	COMPLIB
Essential Software Kits	KITS
Executives Online forum	EXEC
Help with ZiffNet	SUPPORT
MacWEEK News in Brief	MACNEWS
PC Magazine utility	PCMAGUTIL
Product reviews index	INDEX
Games library	PBSARCADE
Take a survey	SURVEY
Tips and Tricks from PC/Computing	TNT
Ziff-Davis Press BookNet	BOOKNET

MONEY MATTERS

On-line Banking

Market Watching

On-line Investing

*Playing the Stock Market:
Simulation Games*

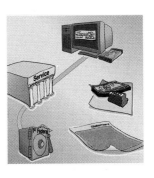

12

With automatic teller machines on every street corner and more

and more banks touting touch-tone telephone banking services, is it any wonder
that you can now handle many money matters on line? After all, banking is a business where dollars and cents are represented by bits and bytes streaming through a
web of electronic networks connecting financial institutions throughout the world.
No doubt, the idea of electronic funds transfers got its start when Western Union
first began wiring money around the United States. Today, you can zap a payment
to just about anyone, anywhere—all through your PC and modem. You can also
keep an eye on Wall Street, getting the latest stock price quotes as if you were on the
trading floor yourself. There are vast libraries of information about companies to
help you evaluate investment opportunities. If the investment looks good, you can
place trade orders directly from your computer.

Some of these financial services are available through the commercial on-line
services you may already want to use. Others are products with on-line connections
of their own, as you'll see throughout this chapter.

On-line Banking

Imagine never having to write a check again—well, almost never again. Two
services, Checkfree and BillPay USA, have gone on line to take the pen and paper
out of check writing. Available to any banking customer, these services enable you
to pay your bills by moving funds electronically from your bank account to those of
your creditors. You don't have to use a particular bank to take advantage of the services, either. You can make a payment from any bank account and pay any individual or corporation in the United States. That's because these services use the same
electronic fund transfer system—The Federal Reserve Automated Clearing House—
that banks use to move money from one organization to another.

ON-LINE BUSINESS NEWS

The on-line world is the first place to turn for up-to-the-minute business and financial news.

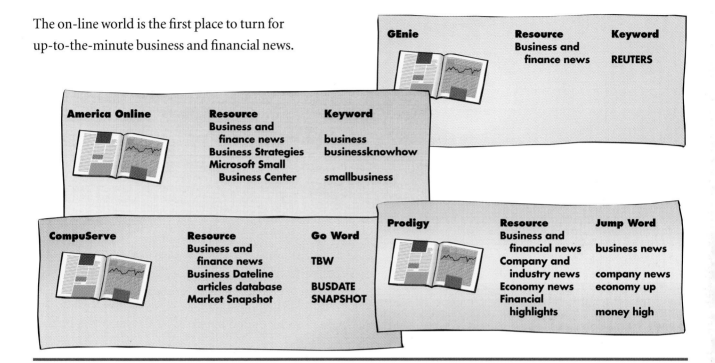

America Online	Resource	Keyword
	Business and finance news	business
	Business Strategies	businessknowhow
	Microsoft Small Business Center	smallbusiness

GEnie	Resource	Keyword
	Business and finance news	REUTERS

CompuServe	Resource	Go Word
	Business and finance news	TBW
	Business Dateline articles database	BUSDATE
	Market Snapshot	SNAPSHOT

Prodigy	Resource	Jump Word
	Business and financial news	business news
	Company and industry news	company news
	Economy news	economy up
	Financial highlights	money high

Using your computer, you tell the electronic bill-paying service which creditors you want to pay. You enter exactly the amount to be paid and the date on which it is to arrive at your creditor's office. You transmit these payment requests to the bill-paying service either through an on-line service or directly to the service via a modem connection. The bill-paying service processes your request and then transfers funds from your account to the creditor's account on the specified date. Businesses of all sizes are equipped to handle these electronic payments, but in some cases, a creditor may not be able to accept electronic payment. When this happens, the bill-paying service prints a check on your bank account and mails it to the creditor. In either case, these payments show up on your bank statement just as ATM transactions and paper checks do.

Electronic bill-paying services are very accurate and efficient—perhaps more so than paper-based checking transactions. The service executes each transaction without any additional processing that could introduce errors. Moreover, once you've paid a

HOW ELECTRONIC BILL-PAYING SERVICES WORK

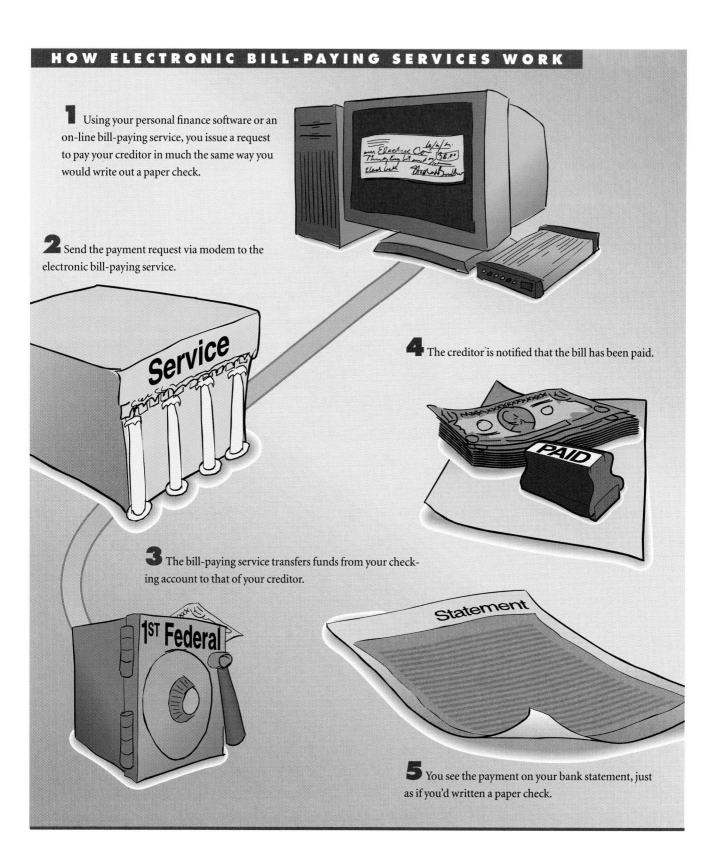

1 Using your personal finance software or an on-line bill-paying service, you issue a request to pay your creditor in much the same way you would write out a paper check.

2 Send the payment request via modem to the electronic bill-paying service.

4 The creditor is notified that the bill has been paid.

3 The bill-paying service transfers funds from your checking account to that of your creditor.

5 You see the payment on your bank statement, just as if you'd written a paper check.

creditor, that payee is on record in your software so that you don't have to reenter the name and address next time. Most of the time, you can select from a list of payees, adjust amounts and payment dates, and send the payment request to the service—all in a fraction of the time it takes to write checks by hand. You can also schedule payments up to a year in advance so that recurring bills, such as your car payment, are automatically paid by the service each month. Best of all, electronic bill-paying services cost no more to use than paper-based transactions and may even save you money. For example, both services discussed below—Checkfree and BillPay USA—charge $9.95 per month to process about 20 or 30 transactions, respectively. If you were to mail 30 checks through the post office, you'd pay $8.70 in postage plus the cost of the checks and applicable bank fees.

BillPay USA (Prodigy, JUMP BILLPAY) works exactly like Checkfree (see below), except that you don't have to use it with any other software program. Instead, you access BillPay USA directly through Prodigy. You enter payment information and then send a payment request to its processing center at Chemical Bank. You can review your payment history and see pending transactions all while connected to Prodigy. If you'd like, you can download this information for use with a number of checkbook management programs, including Managing Your Money, Quicken, Microsoft Money, MacMoney, and virtually any spreadsheet program.

Checkfree (Checkfree Corp., 800-882-5280) was the first electronic bill-paying service widely available to consumers. Checkfree Corporation provides its own checkbook management software, which has a built-in communications package that links to the service. Because of its popularity, two best-selling money management programs, Intuit's Quicken (available for DOS, Windows, and Macintosh computers) and Meca Software's Managing Your Money (available for DOS computers) incorporated the Checkfree service into their packages. Using either of these programs, you enter payments as you normally would, but then use the Checkfree menu option to transmit payment requests directly to the bill-paying service.

MARKET WATCHING

Sitting on the floor of the stock exchange to stay on top of the stock market is hardly more effective than dialing into your on-line service. Every major on-line service— and some bulletin board systems, too—provides continually updated financial news and data. All services offer stock-market quotes, usually updated every 15 minutes that the stock market is open. These *delayed quotes* are much less expensive to access than *real-time stock quotes* that report the current stock price minute-to-minute. Real-time quotes are significantly more expensive to access because of both the value of the current data and the necessary telecommunications links to the trading-floor computers. Some on-line services, such as CompuServe, provide both delayed and real-time quotes.

Quotes are useful for pricing stocks, but investors know that price alone doesn't determine whether you should buy or sell a security. You need lots of additional information, such as company annual reports, pundit opinions, economic indicators, earnings statements, industry analyses, tax information, and the latest business news. You can find all this and more on line. Each service provides the news and information you need to make intelligent investment decisions, plus indexes of leading economic indicators, a database of stock symbols, company profiles, and a bevy of research resources. Three services, however, deserve special mention because they make market watching simple and cost-effective.

Security Objective Services (GEnie, keyword SOS) is a registered investment advisory company that provides market-timing advice and common-stock recommendations, stock-option recommendations, and forecasts of current market trends. The service is designed to give individual investors the information they need to manage a successful portfolio.

StockLink (America Online, keyword STOCKS) is one of the most well-organized, easily accessible business and financial information offerings available. America Online takes full advantage of its graphical interface to bring you company profiles, market indicators, and analyses of the previous day's market activities for all the major stock and commodities exchanges. You can keep track of prices on stocks listed on the various exchanges such as NYSE and NASDAQ, and you can maintain a personal portfolio of up to 100 stocks. This portfolio is automatically updated with current pricing information. In addition to stock information, the service displays mutual-fund prices.

Once you add stocks to your portfolio, you can check their progress to see the total value of your portfolio according to current market prices. StockLink's Market News section keeps you informed of the latest market reports from all the major exchanges.

Strategic Investor (Prodigy, JUMP STRATEGIC INV) is an extra-cost Custom Choice on Prodigy that provides in-depth research resources for personal investors. Strategic Investor includes a database of stocks and mutual-fund information, plus a variety of analyses and chart information. You'll find daily charts of the 50 stocks that show the greatest surge in volume, performance information for most companies listed on the major exchanges, and Stock Hunter, a service that uses a variety of stock valuation techniques to select stocks likely to perform above the market average. A separate service on Prodigy, called Quote Track (JUMP QUOTE TRACK), lets you create lists of up to 50 securities and maintain historical and current price information, much like America Online's StockLink portfolio feature.

On-line Investing

When it's time to act on all that investment analysis and advice, you can buy and sell investments on line, too. CompuServe, America Online, GEnie, and Prodigy all have links to brokerage services that will place your buy and sell orders at the stock exchange. Much like the electronic bill-paying services mentioned earlier, these brokerage services let you enter the stock you'd like to buy or sell, the number of shares you want to exchange, and any specific trade orders. You send a trade order to the brokerage firm's computer, and the computer system processes the order and sends it on to the floor of the exchange. Most orders are automatically cleared through the broker's computer system, but more complex orders are reviewed by a broker before being sent to the exchange. Orders placed while the stock market is open are sent to the trading floor within minutes after you send them to the brokerage firm, while orders placed during the evening or on weekends are executed when the market opens the next business day. Once the trade is complete, the exchange notifies the brokerage firm, which debits or credits your brokerage account and sends you verification of the transaction through the on-line service. To use any of these discount brokerage services, however, you must open a brokerage account with that company. Of course, you can do that on line, too.

Here's a quick list of some of the on-line brokerage services and how you access them:

Charles Schwab Brokerage Services (GEnie, keyword SCHWAB) discounts on-line orders for stocks, bonds, options, and mutual funds by an additional 10 percent off its already discounted rates.

Max Ule's Tickerscreen (CompuServe, GO TKR) offers a wide range of on-line brokerage services and PC-Venture Capital, a program for pairing entrepreneurs with individuals interested in venture-capital enterprises.

PCFN (Prodigy, JUMP PCFN) is one of the largest on-line brokers, claiming to process nearly 10 percent of the daily volume on the New York Stock Exchange. In addition to handling trade orders at discount commissions, PCFN, also known as the PC Financial Network, provides free market reports.

Quick Way Online Brokerage Service (CompuServe, GO QWK) provides a full line of discount brokerage services from Quick & Reilly.

Spear Rees & Co. Online (CompuServe, GO SPEAR) combines discount on-line brokerage services with a toll-free phone order system. Whether you place your order on line or by phone, your on-line portfolio records are automatically updated.

TradePlus (America Online, keyword STOCKLINK) lets you create either hypothetical portfolios to track stocks or brokerage accounts to buy and sell shares of

PLACING BUY AND SELL ORDERS ON LINE

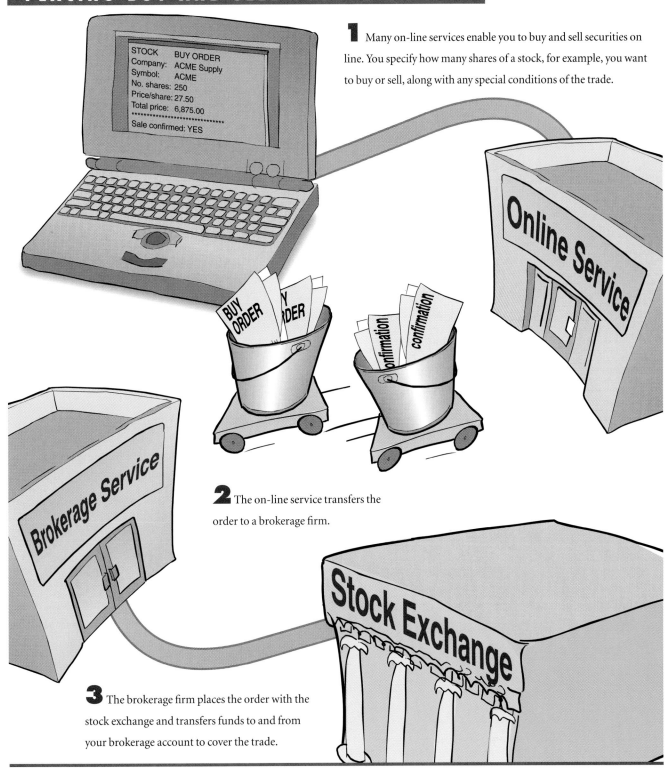

1 Many on-line services enable you to buy and sell securities on line. You specify how many shares of a stock, for example, you want to buy or sell, along with any special conditions of the trade.

STOCK   BUY ORDER
Company: ACME Supply
Symbol: ACME
No. shares: 250
Price/share: 27.50
Total price: 6,875.00
****
Sale confirmed: YES

2 The on-line service transfers the order to a brokerage firm.

3 The brokerage firm places the order with the stock exchange and transfers funds to and from your brokerage account to cover the trade.

stock. A hypothetical portfolio lets you track the performance of stocks and other securities as if you actually owned them.

In addition to the brokerage services provided by the commercial on-line services, there are three software products that combine investment analysis and research with on-line links to the market trading floor. These products build on the expertise of some of the country's largest discount brokerage companies and financial industry pundits. They give you access to databases of financial and business information (including in-depth company reports), provide stock quotes, let you place trade orders on line, and otherwise manage your portfolio. One product, SmartInvestor from Reality Technologies, even helps beginning investors understand the market and devise a portfolio based on the investor's tolerance of market risks and investment goals. Here's what you need to know about each product:

Fidelity Online Xpress, or **FOX** (Fidelity Investments, 800-544-0246) is an on-line trading and investment-tracking program developed jointly by the discount mutual fund company Fidelity Investments and software developer Meca Software. Although FOX doesn't give investment advice, it is a well-designed investment research and trading tool. Through FOX, you can access the information resources of the Dow Jones News/Retrieval, Standard & Poor's, and Telescan databases. You can also access real-time stock quotes and place buy and sell orders through the Fidelity trading system. Because FOX links to Fidelity's computers, you are able to update your Fidelity account information each time you log on to the network. The program costs $119.95, and there are no monthly fees or on-line charges for the basic account or for quote and trading services, except the cost of the phone call. However, you will pay additional fees to access the Dow Jones, Standard & Poor's, and Telescan information.

SmartInvestor (Reality Technologies, 214-387-6055) combines financial planning, research, and investment advice in one package. The program asks a series of questions in order to build your personal financial profile, determining your tolerance to risk and

ON-LINE INVESTING

Investors can stay abreast of their portfolios through these on-line resources.

America Online

Resource	Keyword
Investors' Network	investing
Portfolio management	portfolio
Bulls and Bears stock game	bullsandbears
Stock quotes	stocklink

CompuServe

Resource	Go Word
Stock quotes	BASICQUOTES
Brokerage services	BROKERAGE
Commodity pricing	CPRICE
Company and investment analysis	ANALYZER
	ANALYSIS
Earnings and economic projections	EARNINGS
E*Trade stock market game	ETGAME
Money Magazine Fundwatch Online	MONEYMAG
Index symbol lookup	INDICATORS
	SYMBOLS
Portfolio valuation	PORT
Standard & Poor's company database	S&P
Previous day's market highlights	MARKET

GEnie

Resource	Keyword
Security Objective Services investment advisor	SOS
Quick Way Online brokerage service	QWK
Charles Schwab brokerage service	SCHWAB
Personal finance and investing services	INVESTING
	FINANCE
	MONEY
Closing Stock Quotes	QUOTES

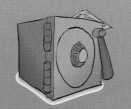

Prodigy

Resource	Jump Word
Discount brokerage services	pcfn
Economic indicators	economic ind
Investors bulletin board	money talk
Kiplinger's Personal Finance magazine	kiplingers
Stock market update	market update
Stock quotes	quote checks
Portfolio tracker	quote track
Online banking	banking
Bill paying	billpay usa

the kinds of investments that will best help you meet your financial objectives. The program then lays out an intelligent investing strategy, including specific stock, bond, and mutual-fund purchase recommendations. Because the program is coupled with an on-line service, you can execute the plan by placing buy and sell orders directly through the program to one of several discount brokerage firms, including PCFN and Quick & Reilly. The on-line service also keeps you up to date on the latest stock quotes, updates its built-in stock and mutual-fund databases as necessary, and alerts you to news that may affect your investments. Smart Investor costs $99.95, plus $9.95 a month for the basic service including the mutual-fund database or $17.95 a month for the mutual-fund database, plus the Standard & Poor's stocks, CD, and money-market databases.

StreetSmart (Charles Schwab, 800-435-4000) is a relatively new product from Charles Schwab Corporation, one of the nation's largest discount brokerage firms. The only Windows-based on-line investment package, StreetSmart lets you track your portfolio, get real-time stock quotes, research investment opportunities, and trade stocks, options, bonds, and mutual funds. You can review your Schwab account on line, and you can check the status of and cancel if necessary any open trade orders. The package sells for $59.00, but you'll get $25.00 off the sales commission the first time you place an order with the program. Schwab also takes 10 percent off commission charges for trades placed on line. There are no connect charges, but you will have to pay a flat monthly fee of $29.00 for access to 20 databases during non-prime-time hours (generally between 6:00 p.m. and 8:00 a.m. local time). If you log on during prime time to use the database, you will be charged by the minute.

PLAYING THE STOCK MARKET: SIMULATION GAMES

If you'd rather not use real money to play the stock market, both CompuServe and America Online have ongoing stock simulation games. You start with a designated amount of money, which you "invest" in the stock market. You buy and sell stocks based on real market prices, and watch your portfolio grow—or not. You compete against other on-line players to see who can build the most valuable portfolio, and, of course, you can chart the performance of your fictitious portfolio against the market performance as a whole.

Bulls and Bears (America Online, keyword BULLSANDBEARS) is a stock-market simulation game in which players buy and sell stocks and options, using real market prices in a race to accumulate the most wealth before the end of the game on the last day of the month. Each player gets a $100,000.00 line of game credit to place initial stock and option orders. You can trade your stocks or options as frequently as you'd like. Trades are executed using the closing price for the market on that day, and your portfolio is updated and your cash balance adjusted. Stock dividends, stock splits, broker's fees, and interest on the cash balance all affect your balance. The top ten players are posted daily, along with your own portfolio position.

E*Trade Stock Market Games (CompuServe, GO ETGAME) are two realistic stock-market games that you play using current stock-market data. Developed and managed by E*Trade Investment Services, one game covers stocks only and the other in-cludes stocks and stock options. Players compete with other CompuServe members to see who can accumulate the most wealth in a month's time. You start either game with a portfolio of $100,000.00 in "game money" to play with. You can trade stocks or options as frequently as you want, and trade orders are executed while the market is open or at the beginning of each trading day. When the order is executed, your portfolio is automatically updated and your cash balance adjusted, including the costs of E*Trade's actual brokerage commission for each trade. The top ten players are posted daily so that you can compare your position with the top ten players anytime. Each month, the holder of the top-performing portfolio receives a $50.00 prize.

INDEX

WHERE CAN YOU BECOME A WHIZ AT WINDOWS, A MASTER AT MACINTOSH AND BATTLE AN ALIEN NATION— ALL BEFORE LUNCH?

Ask questions and exchange opinions with editors and columnists. Make computing even easier - download utilities featured in Ziff-Davis magazines like *PC Magazine*, and *MacUser*.

Choose from thousands of top-rated free and low-cost software programs you can download right to your computer…games, utilities, education, graphics & much more.

Turn to ZiffNet's vast resources for product and price information, plus advice from experts, before you buy.

Get tomorrow's computing news <u>today</u> with *PC Week* and *MacWEEK* online the Friday before they're printed — plus the award-winning international daily newswire, Newsbytes.

Talk directly to product managers and industry leaders from companies like Microsoft,® Lotus,® Apple and IBM®…get in-depth information on just-released products, plus demos of new products.

Instant help for computer problems 24 hours a day. Search quickly for technical tips and get advice from experts and fellow members.

ONLINE, ON ZIFFNET!

FREE Starter Software!

Using ZiffNet Has Never Been Easier.

Sign on to ZiffNet or ZiffNet/Mac (also known as ZMac) the online services all about computing, and join the more than 200,000 computer users who've already discovered the benefits of being part of our community. Even if you've never used a modem before, you'll find that using ZiffNet is an interesting and easy way to learn more about computing.

On ZiffNet and ZMac you can check out our extensive, highly regarded Software Library with thousands of programs - from games, to inexpensive software for home or business, to exclusive ZiffNet custom utilities…be sure you're getting the right products by consulting ZiffNet's buying advice, product reviews and award listings…and call up any article or product review ever printed in the Ziff-Davis magazine archives. And this is just the beginning — you won't find the information and resources ZiffNet offers anywhere else!

Join now and get FREE Starter Software, plus $15 of online time! (see other side for details)

Call 1-800-848-8199 and ask for the ZiffNet private offer for WinCIM or the ZiffNet/Mac private offer for CIM today!

Ziff NET

All about computing online.

Join ZiffNet now and get FREE Starter Software, plus $15 of online time!

Call 1-800-848-8199 today and we'll send you the ZiffNet edition of WinCIM (the Windows version of CompuServe® Information Manager), or CIM for the Macintosh, your ZiffNet ID, password and a $15.00 credit toward online time — all absolutely FREE!

Both versions of CIM use familiar icons and other features to make it easy to use ZiffNet or ZMac and save you money.

In addition, you'll receive a $15.00 credit for online time - use it to get acquainted with the rich services ZiffNet and ZMac have to offer at your own pace.

Hot Shareware and Freeware to Download Today!

As a ZiffNet or ZMac member, you have thousands of top-rated, hand-picked software programs at your fingertips. These programs are all free or inexpensive shareware and freeware. Here's just a sample of the software that you can download today right to your computer.

DOOM	Escape from a 3-D world in this fast-moving "virtual reality" game.
Hexxagon	Strategize on your PC while using familiar board game features.
Slam!	Score big with this fast-paced 3-D hockey game.
Time & Chaos	Take control of your life with this personal information manager.
Jason's File Finder	Find any file across multiple drives with this quick and powerful utility.
System Info Plus	Display information about your system using this convenient reporting utility.
Gates Does Windows	Watch as software mogul Bill Gates cleans and protects your screen.
Mac SEE	This practical utility allows you to read and write to Macintosh formatted disks on a DOS PC.
AddressBook	Print envelopes, labels, Rolodex® cards and even Day Timer® pages with this great application.
ZTerm	A fast, efficient telecommunications program that's simple to use.

So why not join ZiffNet Today? We're waiting to welcome you online right now.

If you're already a CompuServe member, just type GO ZIFFNET or GO ZMAC. It's that easy!